Bullying and Peer Victimization

About the Authors

Amie E. Grills, PhD, is a professor at Boston University's Wheelock College of Education & Human Development. She is a licensed clinical psychologist and researcher whose work has examined the roles of peer (e.g., bullying), familial (e.g., parental stress), and academic (e.g., achievement) variables on the development of youth internalizing difficulties. She also conducts research on risk and resiliency factors among individuals exposed to traumatic events.

Melissa Holt, PhD, is an associate professor at Boston University's Wheelock College of Education & Human Development, and a licensed psychologist. Dr. Holt's research focuses on adolescents' experiences with victimization and identity-based harassment. She has evaluated the overlap among violence exposures, factors that promote resilience among youth exposed to violence, disparities in victimization and its correlates, and the efficacy of school-based prevention programs.

Gerald Reid, PhD, is a licensed psychologist in private practice in Boston, MA, as well as a part-time faculty member at Boston University's Wheelock College of Education. Dr. Reid has conducted research on the topic of bullying in schools. In his practice, Dr. Reid treats patients who have undergone mental health challenges related to interpersonal stressors, such as bullying.

Chelsey Bowman, PhD, is a postdoctoral psychology fellow at Children's National Hospital in Washington, DC. Dr. Bowman's research interests include understanding the impact of a range of victimization forms, including bullying, on the health and wellbeing of youth and college students. Clinically, Dr. Bowman provides evidence-based treatments to youth and their families for chronic and acute medical and psychiatric conditions.

Advances in Psychotherapy – Evidence-Based Practice

Series Editor
Danny Wedding, PhD, MPH, Professor Emeritus, University of Missouri–Saint Louis, MO

Associate Editors
Jonathan S. Comer, PhD, Professor of Psychology and Psychiatry, Director of Mental Health Interventions and Technology (MINT) Program, Center for Children and Families, Florida International University, Miami, FL
J. Kim Penberthy, PhD, ABPP, Professor of Psychiatry & Neurobehavioral Sciences, University of Virginia, Charlottesville, VA
Kenneth E. Freedland, PhD, Professor of Psychiatry and Psychology, Washington University School of Medicine, St. Louis, MO
Linda C. Sobell, PhD, ABPP, Professor, Center for Psychological Studies, Nova Southeastern University, Ft. Lauderdale, FL

The basic objective of this series is to provide therapists with practical, evidence-based treatment guidance for the most common disorders seen in clinical practice – and to do so in a reader-friendly manner. Each book in the series is both a compact "how-to" reference on a particular disorder for use by professional clinicians in their daily work and an ideal educational resource for students as well as for practice-oriented continuing education.

The most important feature of the books is that they are practical and easy to use: All are structured similarly and all provide a compact and easy-to-follow guide to all aspects that are relevant in real-life practice. Tables, boxed clinical "pearls," marginal notes, and summary boxes assist orientation, while checklists provide tools for use in daily practice.

Continuing Education Credits

Psychologists and other healthcare providers may earn five continuing education credits for reading the books in the *Advances in Psychotherapy* series and taking a multiple-choice exam. This continuing education program is a partnership of Hogrefe Publishing and the National Register of Health Service Psychologists. Details are available at https://www.hogrefe.com/us/cenatreg

The National Register of Health Service Psychologists is approved by the American Psychological Association to sponsor continuing education for psychologists. The National Register maintains responsibility for this program and its content.

Advances in Psychotherapy – Evidence-Based Practice, Volume 47

Bullying and Peer Victimization

Amie E. Grills
Wheelock College of Education & Human Development,
Boston University, MA

Melissa Holt
Wheelock College of Education & Human Development,
Boston University, MA

Gerald Reid
Wheelock College of Education & Human Development,
Boston University, MA

Chelsey Bowman
Children's National Hospital, Washington, DC

Library of Congress of Congress Cataloging in Publication information for the print version of this book is available via the Library of Congress Marc Database under the Library of Congress Control Number 2022940899

Library and Archives Canada Cataloguing in Publication
Title: Bullying and peer victimization / Amie E. Grills (Wheelock College of Education & Human Development, Boston University, MA), Melissa Holt (Wheelock College of Education & Human Development, Boston University, MA), Gerald Reid (Wheelock College of Education & Human Development, Boston University, MA), Chelsey Bowman (Children's National Hospital, Washington, DC).
Names: Grills, Amie E., author. | Holt, Melissa K., author. | Reid, Gerald (Lecturer in counseling psychology), author. | Bowman, Chelsey (Ph. D. in psychology), author.
Series: Advances in psychotherapy--evidence-based practice ; v. 47.
Description: Series statement: Advances in psychotherapy--evidence-based practice ; volume 47 | Includes bibliographical references.
Identifiers: Canadiana (print) 20220273030 | Canadiana (ebook) 20220273081 | ISBN 9780889374089 (softcover) | ISBN 9781616764081 (PDF) | ISBN 9781613344088 (EPUB)
Subjects: LCSH: Bullying. | LCSH: Bullying—Psychological aspects. | LCSH: Cyberbullying. | LCSH: Bullies. | LCSH: Victims of bullying.
Classification: LCC BF637.B85 G75 2022 | DDC 302.34/3—dc23

© 2023 by Hogrefe Publishing
www.hogrefe.com

The authors and publisher have made every effort to ensure that the information contained in this text is in accord with the current state of scientific knowledge, recommendations, and practice at the time of publication. In spite of this diligence, errors cannot be completely excluded. Also, due to changing regulations and continuing research, information may become outdated at any point. The authors and publisher disclaim any responsibility for any consequences which may follow from the use of information presented in this book.

Registered trademarks are not noted specifically as such in this publication. The use of descriptive names, registered names, and trademarks does not imply, even in the absence of a specific statement, that such names are exempt from the relevant protective laws and regulations and therefore free for general use.

The cover image is an agency photo depicting models. Use of the photo on this publication does not imply any connection between the content of this publication and any person depicted in the cover image.
Cover image: © SeventyFour – iStock.com

PUBLISHING OFFICES

USA:	Hogrefe Publishing Corporation, 44 Merrimac St., Suite 207, Newburyport, MA 01950 Phone (978) 255 3700; E-mail customersupport@hogrefe.com
EUROPE:	Hogrefe Publishing GmbH, Merkelstr. 3, 37085 Göttingen, Germany Phone +49 551 99950 0, Fax +49 551 99950 111; E-mail publishing@hogrefe.com

SALES & DISTRIBUTION

USA:	Hogrefe Publishing, Customer Services Department, 30 Amberwood Parkway, Ashland, OH 44805 Phone (800) 228 3749, Fax (419) 281 6883; E-mail customersupport@hogrefe.com
UK:	Hogrefe Publishing, c/o Marston Book Services Ltd., 160 Eastern Ave., Milton Park, Abingdon, OX14 4SB Phone +44 1235 465577, Fax +44 1235 465556; E-mail direct.orders@marston.co.uk
EUROPE:	Hogrefe Publishing, Merkelstr. 3, 37085 Göttingen, Germany Phone +49 551 99950 0, Fax +49 551 99950 111; E-mail publishing@hogrefe.com

OTHER OFFICES

CANADA:	Hogrefe Publishing Corporation, 82 Laird Drive, East York, Ontario M4G 3V1
SWITZERLAND:	Hogrefe Publishing, Länggass-Strasse 76, 3012 Bern

No part of this book may be reproduced, stored in a retrieval system or transmitted, in any form or by any means, electronic, mechanical, photocopying, microfilming, recording or otherwise, without written permission from the publisher.

Printed and bound in the USA

ISBN 978-0-88937-408-9 (print) • ISBN 978-1-61676-408-1 (PDF) • ISBN 978-1-61334-408-8 (EPUB)
http://doi.org/10.1027/00408-000

Acknowledgments

This book is dedicated to the children and families who have been affected by bullying and victimization. We would also like to acknowledge the researchers, clinicians, educators, practitioners, and legislators who have worked tirelessly to understand and prevent bullying, enact antibullying policies at the school and state levels, and address consequences of bullying. Finally, we would like to thank the Hogrefe team for their continual support for this important project.

To my husband, Nate, for sharing in the highs and lows of life at my side, raising our amazing children together, and making me laugh at the end of each day with your ridiculous dance moves and longwinded stories. To my children – how I love watching each of you growing into the incredible humans you are. Francesca, you are so thoughtful, caring, and funny – you approach each day like a challenge to conquer (look out F1!). Luciana, you are full of kindness and have the most positive and joyful spirit I have ever known – you approach each day ready to share that with everyone around you (unless they try to mess with your mama!). Conrad, you have so much creativity and bring it to everything you do – you approach each day eager to try something new (just not mashed potatoes!). To my coauthor and dearest friend and colleague, Melissa – looking forward to many years of RAM, MBT, and CPP. And finally, for my dad, who demonstrated for all of us how to lead a life full of grace and benevolence and who was cheering me on as I completed this project as he had all my endeavors – you are missed every day.

A.G.

To Amie, the most spectacular of coauthors, colleagues, and friends – I am forever grateful for the initial invitation to collaborate, which led to all that has followed. To my family: Lowell, who reminds me to slow down; Emmeline, whose joyful way of being brightens my days; Katherine, whose delicious meals nourish me; and Nicholas, for our discussions of education and humanity.

M.H.

Thank you to my family and mentors. Your support and encouragement to develop into the man I am today will always motivate me to do my best to support and encourage others.

G.R.

Mom, thanks for everything.

C.B.

Contents

Acknowledgments v

1	**Description**	1
1.1	Terminology	2
1.2	Definitions	2
1.3	Epidemiology and Course	3
1.4	High-Risk Subgroups	5
1.5	Differential Diagnosis	5
1.6	Correlates/Comorbidities	6
1.6.1	Mental and Physical Health Correlates	6
1.7	Summary	10

2	**Theories and Models**	11
2.1	Social-Ecological Theory	11
2.2	Social Learning Theory	12
2.3	Group Dynamics	14
2.4	Cognitive Factors	15
2.5	Individual Factors for Bullies	17
2.6	Individual Factors for Victims	19
2.7	Theories Specifically Focused on Cyberbullying	20
2.8	Summary	21

3	**Diagnosis and Treatment Indicators**	23
3.1	Assessment of Bullying Experiences	23
3.1.1	Self-Report Survey Assessments of Bullying and Victimization Experiences	23
3.1.2	Others' Reports of Bullying and Victimization Experiences ...	25
3.1.3	Observations	26
3.1.4.	Interviews	27
3.2	Assessment of Correlates or Difficulties Commonly Associated With Bullying	28

4	**Treatment**	33
4.1	Methods of Treatment	33
4.2	Mechanisms of Action	33
4.3	Efficacy	34
4.4	Variations and Combinations of Methods	35
4.4.1	Olweus Bullying Prevention Program (OBPP)	35
4.4.2	Kiusaamista Vastaan (KiVa)	38
4.4.3	Second Step Social-Emotional Learning	40
4.4.4	Key Elements Across Effective Programs	42
4.5	Problems in Carrying Out the Treatments	43
4.6	Summary	44

5	**Case Vignette**	45
6	**Further Reading**	49
7	**References**	51
8	**Appendix: Tools and Resources**	63

1

Description

Maria is a 12-year-old girl who just started seventh grade at a new middle school. She is vibrant, creative, and caring. She tries hard to make friends over the first few weeks of school, but no one invites her to sit with them at lunch or to hang out after school. One day a group of girls ask her to sit with them at lunch and Maria is thrilled! They tell her that they know a boy who likes her. Maria is excited by the news of a potential crush and even more excited to be sitting with a group of potential friends. The ringleader of the girls encourages Maria to message the boy on Instagram and even gives Maria the boy's Instagram account name. At night, Maria excitedly messages the boy's account and to her surprise he immediately responds. Over the next few weeks, she begins messaging him every night. He encourages her to share her secrets and dares her to do things that Maria does not feel quite right doing, but does anyway for fear of losing her new friends. At school, this boy never seems to notice or acknowledge her, but online he says this makes their relationship even more special. A few weeks later, Maria walks into English class and feels like everyone is whispering about her. She tries to focus on the teacher, but she hears two students giggling and saying her name. Between classes, Maria returns to her locker and finds that it has been vandalized. Someone has taped a piece of paper that says "Maria is a slut" in large red letters. Scared, crying, and feeling helpless, Maria rips the sign off her locker and runs to the bathroom. Hiding in a stall, she hears two of the girls she sits with at lunch discussing the day's drama. They are giggling at the fact that they convinced Maria that a boy had a crush on her when in fact they created a fake Instagram account and pretended to be the boy. Maria realizes that the girls she thought were her friends, were actually the ones talking to her on Instagram. Worse, they were sending screenshots of the messages to the whole grade.

Stories like the one above are all too common and reflect the pressing need to address bullying – the full story, including interventions, is provided in Chapter 5. Over the past decade there has been an explosion of media attention on youth bullying. News articles have focused on individual youth who have been bullied at school and/or online and have been driven to the depths of despair. Stories about youth who were perceived as "different" because of their accent, gender identity, skin color, sexual orientation, or interests, and who experienced verbal and physical assaults, online taunting, and other forms of harassment, frequently make headlines. Antibullying laws now exist in all US states, and lawsuits related to bullying have become increasingly common. While always devastating, the stories are rarely as simple as the media coverage. In fact, peer victimization and bullying among youth are typically quite complex interpersonal phenomenon that are situated within rapidly shifting developmental stages. Furthermore, with the advent of social media, bullying can quickly start and spread virally with little to no oversight from parents, teachers, and/or administrators. Although in-person bullying remains the most common, cyberbullying incidents add complications, such as the swift spreading to entire friend groups, grades, and even schools.

In order to address and prevent youth bullying effectively, it is necessary to have a clear understanding of definitions, prevalence, correlates, theoretical perspectives, and available assessments and interventions. In the subsequent chapters, each of these areas will be discussed.

1.1 Terminology

Unfortunately, youth can experience and witness many types of victimization during childhood. They may experience abuse or neglect at the hands of their parents or guardians (see the 2nd edition of volume 4 in this series, *Childhood Maltreatment* by Wekerle et al., 2019) or by their siblings (sibling abuse). They may witness domestic violence between adults within their home (see volume 23 in this series, *Growing Up With Domestic Violence* by Jaffe et al., 2012) and in their community (community violence). They may experience abuse within a dating relationship (see coming volume in this series, *Dating Violence* by Franco et al., in press) or be sexually assaulted by a peer, family member, or stranger (see volume 17 in this series, *Sexual Violence* by Holcomb, 2010). They can also be victimized by friends, classmates, or peers; whether in person or online, this form of victimization is known as *peer victimization*.

> **Bullying can occur at any age, and frequently has negative consequences for health and wellbeing**

When peer victimization is characterized by intentionality, repetition, and a power imbalance, it is commonly referred to as *bullying*. Decades of research highlights that peer victimization and bullying can occur at any age and can negatively impact an individual's health and well-being. Indeed, studies have shown that bullying occurs among youth (e.g., Modecki et al., 2014), college students (e.g., Lund & Ross, 2017), and adults in the workplace (e.g., Samnani & Singh, 2012). However, this book focuses specifically on peer victimization and bullying experiences among youth. Appendix 1 includes a list of several websites, apps, and events that can be referenced for additional information and updates.

1.2 Definitions

> **Bullying can take many forms from physical assault to alienation to social media attacks**

Terms such as *teasing* (e.g., "Your mom's so fat…") and *rough-housing* (e.g., play-wrestling) have long been used to describe common interactions among youth (Roberts & Morotti, 2000). However, over the past 40 years, there has been increasing recognition of the fact that these interactions may be harmful or maladaptive, and that they may lead to detrimental outcomes. From research studies to popular press, a variety of labels emerged (e.g., peer victimization, bullying, taunting, mobbing, cyberbullying) to refer to forms of teasing that are unwelcome. Oftentimes, attempts to identify markers for determining when these behaviors deviated from normative, nonhurtful youth experiences have been made and they typically include: (1) the manner in which the behaviors were delivered, (2) their intensity, (3) their frequency or incidence, and (4) the target's perception of them (Roberts & Morotti, 2000). In addition, subgroupings of peer victimization experiences are sometimes described, for instance to distinguish between direct or openly confrontational (e.g., physical or verbal assaults), indirect or covertly manipulative (e.g., ostracism, social manipulation), and technology-delivered bullying (e.g., via email, text messages, internet sites; Mynard & Joseph, 2000).

An early comprehensive definition emerged after years of work studying youth in Norway by Dan Olweus, who defined bullying as repeated exposure to *negative actions* (i.e., an intentional attempt or infliction of discomfort which may take the form of physical contact, words, facial expressions and gestures, intentional defiance of one's wishes or requests, or social isolation and exclusion) *from at least one other person over time*, with an *imbalance of power*, real or perceived, between the perpetrator and target (Olweus, 1993). More recently, the United States Centers for Disease Control and Prevention released a similar definition of bullying that states, "Bullying is any unwanted aggressive behavior(s) by another youth or group of youths who are not siblings or current dating partners that involves an observed or perceived power imbalance and is repeated multiple times or is highly likely to be repeated. Bullying may inflict harm or distress on the targeted youth including physical, psychological, social, or educational harm" (Gladden et al., 2014).

Definitions of bullying have converged and generally reflect: repeated negative actions inflicted over time from another person with greater power

A separate set of terms has emerged for describing youth who are involved in bullying, such as: (1) bully (an individual who solely perpetrates acts against other[s]); (2) victim (an individual who is the recipient of bullying behaviors); (3) bully–victim (an individual who both perpetrates acts against others and is the recipient of bullying behaviors); (4) bystander (an individual who is not directly involved as a bully or a victim, but who witnesses such behaviors); and (5) comparison (an individual who does not report being involved in bullying behaviors). While these terms often emerge in research studies interested in examining categorical distinctions, it is likely that bullying behaviors fall along a continuum and vary across contexts. Further, research has demonstrated that bullying involvement roles are not static, but that students' roles can fluctuate throughout their schooling due to a number of factors and transitions (e.g., Kljakovic & Hunt, 2016).

Youth can be involved in bullying as bullies, victims, bully-victims, or bystanders; and their involvement and roles can change over time

1.3   Epidemiology and Course

Prevalence estimates of peer victimization vary greatly as a function of the definition and inclusion criteria employed (Furlong et al., 2010). It may be that broader or less well-defined terms contribute to discrepancies in reported behaviors. For example, students who were provided with a definition of bullying and repeated exposure to the word "bully" reported significantly less bullying behavior compared to students whose surveys did not include the word "bully" (Kert et al., 2010). Therefore, in attempting to evaluate behaviors

> **Approximately 10–25% of students report being bullied at school**

> **Bullying is most frequent during early adolescence**

consistent with peer victimization, it is important to provide a clear definition of terms at the outset to facilitate consistent understanding.

In the United States, rates of bullying from the *2015 Youth Risk Behavior Surveillance* revealed that 20.2% of high school students reported being bullied on school property and 15.5% reported being cyberbullied (Kann et al., 2016). National data assessing victimization among middle and high school students (aged 12–18) similarly found that 22% of students reported being bullied at school and 7% reported being cyberbullied (Robers et al., 2015). In younger children (grades 3–6), bullying on most days or more was reported by 8–10% of US and Australian students surveyed; however, 20–28% of students reported being victimized once a week or more (Perry et al., 1988).

Overall, examination of age effects often reveals that bullying peaks in the early middle school years, and then decreases as youth advance grades (Furlong et al., 2010). However, it is important to note that some researchers now believe that bullying-like behaviors do not stop, but rather take new forms during later adolescence (e.g., in the form of teen dating violence or workplace harassment; Bellmore et al., 2017). Indeed, research has supported the existence of a *bully-sexual violence pathway*, whereby engaging in bullying perpetration and homophobic teasing has been found to predict later sexual violence perpetration by boys (Espelage, Basile, et al., 2015).

Potential differences in prevalence estimates have also been explored with respect to a range of sociodemographic characteristics, including gender, race/ethnicity, disability status, and sexual orientation. With regard to gender, a meta-analysis of 153 studies found only a small effect supporting the notion that boys were more likely to be victims of bullying than girls (Cook et al., 2010). That said, the *type* of bullying experienced may differ by gender, such that boys are more likely to experience overt or physical acts of victimization, while girls experience more covert acts (Chester et al., 2017). Moreover, covert relational bullying among girls, such as social exclusion or rumor spreading, appears to become more common as they approach late childhood (Wang et al., 2009). In all, these findings point to the need to attend to how bullying involvement might manifest itself differently among boys and girls, with attention to developmental stage. Future research should also assess experiences of nonbinary and transgender adolescents; the limited research to date on gender diverse youths has highlighted that transgender adolescents report more peer victimization than their cisgender peers (Johns et al., 2019).

Fewer studies have examined how bullying involvement might vary by race/ethnicity. The *2015 Youth Risk Behavior Surveillance* found that White students in the United States reported higher rates of bullying on school property and being cyberbullied than Black and Hispanic students (Kann et al., 2016), although there are inconsistent findings due to differences in survey methods and participant characteristics. For example, racial and ethnic minority youth reported lower rates of being bullied despite reporting similar or significantly greater rates of experiencing bullying behaviors than their white peers (Lai & Kao, 2018). A study of Canadian youth found that whether an individual is part of the majority or minority group within their community and the amount of diversity in their community were more strongly related to bullying involvement, demonstrating that context can also matter (Schumann et al., 2013). Given findings like these, it is important that those seeking to understand bullying behaviors consider the ways in which bullying is measured and the context in which the bullying occurs.

The prevalence of bullying also varies depending on the type. For instance, in a US-based national study, rates were 20.8% for physical, 53.6% for verbal, and 51.4% for social manifestations of bullying (Wang et al., 2009). Studies on cyberbullying have also found widely ranging rates, from roughly 10-35% for victimization and 5-20% for perpetration (e.g., Kann et al., 2016; Wang et al., 2009). Overall, many youths are directly involved in peer victimization experiences on a regular basis during their childhood and adolescent years. Furthermore, due to the intimidation often associated with peer victimization, reported rates are often considered underestimated (Casey-Cannon et al., 2001).

Prevalence studies have shown us that bullying is a significant public health problem that affects far too many students each year

1.4 High-Risk Subgroups

Beyond demographic characteristics, there are also groups of youth who are at particularly high risk for bullying involvement. For example, students with disabilities are more likely to be involved in bullying than students without disabilities (e.g., Rose & Gage, 2017). Evidence suggests that the association between disability status and bullying involvement is nuanced, in that factors such as the nature of the disability and the type and visibility of the received special education influence the strength of the relation (Swearer et al., 2012).

Youth with disabilities and those who identify as LGBTQ are at particular risk for experiencing bullying

Lesbian, gay, bisexual, transgender, and queer (LGBTQ) youth also are at higher risk for bullying involvement, particularly in terms of victimization (e.g., Kosciw et al., 2009). For instance, in a sample of high school students, 10.1% of lesbian/bisexual girls reported being victimized at school 10 or more times in the past year compared to 1.1% of heterosexual girls (Bontempo & D'Augelli, 2002). Similarly, in this same sample 24.0% of gay/bisexual boys reported in-school victimization occurring 10 or more times in the past year in contrast to 2.7% of heterosexual boys. Increased risk among LGBTQ youth has also been supported through a recent meta-analysis in which sexual minority youth were 1.7 times more likely to be physically assaulted at school and 2.4 times more likely to miss school due to fear than their heterosexual peers (Friedman et al., 2011). LGBTQ youths living in rural communities or those with lower adult educational attainment, as well as those in geographic areas with higher rates of LGBTQ assault hate crimes may be especially at risk for victimization (Hatzenbuehler et al., 2015; Kosciw et al., 2009). In sum, research clearly demonstrates that bullying disproportionately affects certain groups of students and require awareness and careful consideration among school personnel.

1.5 Differential Diagnosis

While there is not a unique diagnosis in the present *Diagnostic and Statistical Manual of Mental Disorders* (DSM-5; APA, 2013) for bullying behaviors, it may be valuable for practitioners, teachers, parents and others to understand distinctions between these behaviors and other mental health concerns that share signs and symptoms.

Bullying behaviors may overlap with several externalizing disorders. For example, impulsivity is a hallmark symptom of attention-deficit/hyperactivity disorder (ADHD). However, youth with ADHD experience a pervasive set of clustered hyperactive/impulsive and/or inattentive symptoms (e.g., excessive talking, behaving as if driven by a motor, poor focus) that are present in multiple domains (e.g., home and school), inconsistent with their developmental level, and have been present prior to age 12 (APA, 2013; Grills & Holt, 2017).

Likewise, bullying behaviors may be part of the diagnostic picture for youth who meet criteria for a disorder from the disruptive, impulse-control, or conduct disorders section of DSM-5 (e.g., conduct, intermittent explosive, and oppositional defiant disorders; APA, 2013). However, in each of these cases, a range of additional symptoms are necessary for diagnosis (e.g., for oppositional defiant disorder symptoms cut across three areas, including angry/irritable mood, argumentative/defiant behavior, and vindictiveness), as are a heightened frequency and intensity of symptoms, and the symptoms must result in clinically significant impairment in key functional domains (APA, 2013; Grills & Holt, 2017). Thus, bullying behaviors can be a feature of these disruptive disorders, and their presence may be a signal for further evaluation.

Victims of bullying may also demonstrate behaviors consistent with other disorders depicted in the DSM-5. For example, a victim may express hopelessness (a symptom of a depressive disorder) or fearfulness (a symptom of an anxiety disorder); however, those signs alone would not warrant a clinical diagnosis. Rather, a thorough assessment would be required to determine if the child had developed the cluster of symptoms and other criteria consistent with diagnosis of one of these internalizing disorders. Indeed, internalizing difficulties like anxiety and depression are commonly present for victims and may, at least initially, mask the underlying cause. Given the frequency with which victimized youth report comorbid disorders (see Section 1.6.1: Mental and Physical Health Correlates), evaluation of these domains may be critical as soon as any sign of bullying becomes apparent. Likewise, an evaluation of experiences with bullying should be included in assessment batteries for youth presenting with other primary concerns.

> Bullying is not a formal DSM-5 diagnosis, but bullying and related behaviors may be symptoms of other disorders

1.6 Correlates/Comorbidities

1.6.1 Mental and Physical Health Correlates

Studies have found a range of mental and physical health correlates associated with bullying involvement. Typically, bullies are depicted as evidencing greater externalizing behaviors (e.g., aggression, impulsivity), whereas victims are depicted as evidencing increased internalizing difficulties (e.g., social and emotional distress). However, as described below, it is important to note that these distinctions do not uniformly hold true – that is, both bullies and victims

> Mental and physical health correlates have been found among youth classified as bullies, victims, or bully-victims

experience a range of comorbid difficulties that encompass externalizing and internalizing domains.

Perpetrators of Bullying
For youth who engage in bullying, other aggressive behaviors are commonly present. For example, bullying can be associated with a range of other externalizing behaviors (e.g., increased rates of gang involvement, bringing weapons to school, and fighting; Fitzpatrick et al., 2007), and disorders (e.g., attention-deficit/hyperactivity disorder, oppositional defiant disorder, conduct disorder; e.g., Unnever & Cornell, 2003).

Learning and internalizing difficulties have also been found among youth who engage in bullying. For example, because some children with learning disabilities have poor social skills, misinterpret verbal communication, and display aggressive tendencies, they may take on a bullying role in the classroom (Kaukiainen et al., 2002). Bullying perpetration has also been associated with depressive symptoms, perhaps due to irritability and emotion regulation difficulties (Wang et al., 2011), as well as later social anxiety (Pabian & Vandebosch, 2016).

Substance use, including involvement with alcohol/drugs (e.g., Kelly et al., 2015), and cigarette smoking (Morris et al., 2006) have also been reported as correlates among bullies. In a prospective study of Finnish males, bullying perpetration at age 8 predicted illicit drug use at age 18 (Niemelä et al., 2011). Furthermore, students who bully others are more likely to engage in sexual risk-taking behaviors, including having casual sex and having sex under the influence of illicit substances compared to their nonbullying peers (Holt, Matjasko, et al., 2013).

Victims of Bullying
Research has also identified a number of negative physical and mental health correlates among victims of bullying. Anxiety is one of the most common features of victims of bullying, especially social anxiety (Hawker & Boulton, 2000). Depression and related difficulties, including poor self-worth, suicidal ideation, and suicidal behaviors have also been commonly reported among bullied youth (Austin & Joseph, 1996; Grills & Ollendick, 2000; Kaltiala-Heino et al., 1999; Olweus, 1993; van Geel et al., 2014; Wang et al., 2011). It is important to note that research supports an *association* between bullying and suicidal behaviors, but not a *causal* relationship (Holt et al., 2015). Unfortunately, these same internalizing symptoms may also promote continued bullying from others. For example, looking across several longitudinal studies, Reijntjes and colleagues' (2010) meta-analysis found that peer victimization and internalizing problems have a reciprocal relationship, in which internalizing problems can both contribute to and follow victimization (Reijntjes, Kamphuis, Prinzie, & Telch, 2010).

Physical health correlates have also been reported among youth involved in bullying (e.g., Holt et al., 2014). Gini and Pozzoli (2013) conducted a meta-analysis to examine the relationships between psychosomatic complaints and involvement in bullying. Students who were bullied were at least two times more likely to endorse psychosomatic complaints than their peers who were not bullied. Thus, repeated exposure to bullying experiences may take a toll on a student's physical health, as well as their emotional well-being. Notably, students who experience multiple forms of victimization (i.e., relational, physical, etc.), or victimization across multiple contexts (e.g., cyber and school) are at even greater risk for these negative outcomes (Schneider et al., 2012; Wang et al., 2010).

Comparisons by Bullying Involvement Subgroups

Bullying involvement role comparisons (i.e., victim-only, bully-only, bully–victim, and comparison) have also been conducted to explore whether particular subgroups of youth involved in bullying are at greater risk for specific mental health comorbidities. Summarizing across much of this work, Hawker and Boulton's (2000) meta-analysis of studies published between 1978 and 1997 revealed greater levels of psychosocial adjustment problems (e.g., social and generalized anxiety, depression) among victims than nonvictims. In a separate meta-analysis, being involved in bullying in any form (i.e., bully, bully–victim, victim) was associated with increased suicidal ideation and behaviors (Holt et al., 2014). Bully–victims, too, have been found to evidence marked psychosocial impairment (e.g., Kaltiala-Heino et al., 1999; Klomek et al., 2007) and risk for alcohol and drug use (Radliff et al., 2012).

Longitudinal Studies

Longitudinal studies have found that the negative correlates associated with bullying experiences can persist into adulthood

The negative correlates of peer victimization during youth can also persist into adulthood. Internalizing difficulties, including anxiety, depression, and psychosomatic complaints, in adulthood have been particularly linked with being bullied in childhood (Gini & Pozzoli, 2013; Holt et al., 2014). As an example, even after controlling for childhood psychiatric disorders and family hardships, youth who were bullied had a higher prevalence of a number of anxiety disorders as young adults compared to their nonbullied peers (Copeland et al., 2013). In an early study, Olweus (1993) found that adult males (age 23) who were victimized in grades 9–11, but no longer continued to be so, were more likely to evidence symptoms of depression and low self-worth, and the degree of adult depressive symptoms endorsed was strongly related to the severity of childhood victimization reported. Beyond internalizing difficulties, associations with other long-term difficulties have been noted (e.g., borderline personality disorder, psychiatric treatment, physical complaints, poor functioning in relationships) (e.g., Holt et al., 2014; Sigurdson et al., 2014).

Long-term difficulties have also been reported among perpetrators of bullying, including antisocial behavior and criminal involvement in adulthood (e.g., Olweus, 2011; Sourander et al., 2011), depression, unemployment, poor job functioning, and drug use (Klomek et al., 2008; Sigurdson et al., 2014).

Social Correlates

Associations between peer victimization and social correlates such as isolation, lack of peer support, lower social acceptance, and perceived social competence have been noted (Grills & Ollendick, 2000; Wright & Li, 2013). For example, in a three-year longitudinal study, individuals who were classified as bullies in both their childhood and adolescence ("stable bullies") were more disliked by their peers, displayed more aggression than their peers, and were less likely to be nominated as a friend. In contrast "stable victims" – individuals who were classified as victims in both their childhood and adolescence – received significantly higher scores in being disliked compared to individuals who were classified as only victims of bullying in childhood (Scholte et al., 2007). These findings highlight the importance of considering the timing and stability of bullying because more negative social outcomes may emerge over time. Gender dynamics may also be an important consideration, as evidenced by Veenstra and colleagues' (2010) finding that bullies in elementary and middle school tended to target same-sex victims who were socially rejected by their peers. Further, bullies were more often rejected by their same-sex peers, but not opposite-sex peers, likely because bullies were not perceived as a threat by opposite-sex peers (Veenstra et al., 2010).

Social correlates also may serve a positive role for students involved in peer victimization. For example, social support from peers and/or families may buffer the deleterious effects of being bullied (e.g., Rothon et al., 2011). Additionally, among youth who are socially rejected, peer-valued characteristics such as wealth and athletic ability moderate the relationship with peer victimization. In all, these findings highlight the nuanced relationship between victimization and social correlates/outcomes. Understanding the role of social factors and relationships that may have precipitated victimization, as well as adverse social outcomes deriving from involvement with bullying, can help identify appropriate interventions.

Social factors associated with bullying can have positive (e.g., support from friends, teachers) or negative (e.g., rejection from peers) effects

School and Academic Correlates

The potential influence of bullying on academic performance is unclear (e.g., Cook et al. 2010; Nakamoto & Schwartz, 2009). It might be that other contextual variables influence whether academic performance is affected for victims. For instance, youth who have adequate social support despite experiencing bullying may be protected from experiencing academic (or other) difficulties (Rothon et al., 2011). Psychological functioning might also play a role; for instance, depressive symptoms may mediate the association between victimization and academic competence (Juvonen et al., 2000). Thus, while academic performance may not always be affected among bullied youth it is certainly a potential correlate and one that may be noticed by teachers or families even before they are aware of a child being bullied.

Other difficulties specific to school have also been reported among bullied youth, including school refusal and avoidance/absenteeism (Salmon et al., 2000), as well as reported unhappiness or fear about school (Bernstein & Watson, 1997). These varied school-based difficulties likely reflect the child's desire to avoid school and thus, victimization. However, increased school absenteeism may lead to additional social and education difficulties for youths and may not decrease bullying as students take to online platforms.

School difficulties, including absenteeism, fear, refusal to attend, and grade decline, may be indicators of bullying

Studies of youths who bully others generally reveal poorer academic achievement (Cook et al., 2010; Ma et al., 2009; Nansel et al., 2001), as well as more negative perceptions of their relationships with teachers (Bacchini et al., 2009)

Taken together, there is some support for the association between bullying involvement and academic functioning, with inconsistent findings emerging for the experiences of victims of bullying and more consistent support for the relation between perpetrating bullying behaviors and academic indicators.

1.7 Summary

In sum, school-based peer victimization affects many youths, with some subgroups at particularly high risk for experiencing or perpetrating such behaviors. Negative physical and mental health outcomes have been reported among youth involved in these behaviors, whether as bullies, victims, or both. Notably, involvement in peer victimization (as a target, perpetrator, or both) is associated not only with concurrent deleterious effects on functioning in multiple domains, but also with effects that persist into adulthood. Taken together, these findings underscore the critical importance of addressing peer victimization within schools.

2

Theories and Models

This chapter provides theoretical and empirical perspectives that offer potential explanations for why bullying occurs. Within any relationship, there can be harm done within the context of a power differential. Differences in power can occur in almost any form, depending on context (Farrell et al., 2015). For instance, a mild-mannered young boy of small stature can feel weaker, or even scared, in comparison to a stronger, larger, and more hostile peer. A shy child with few friends may feel intimidated by a popular child who has a large social group. The contrast between a majority and minority group can also set the stage for power dynamics to emerge, as members of the minority group feel isolated or outnumbered. Even qualities of being smarter, wealthier, or more "talented" than others can constitute a power differential. Problems emerge when one's sense of power contributes to malevolent behavior, which is the case with bullying.

> Power dynamics are important to consider for any relational difficulties, including bullying

There are various pathways by which a child can ultimately become involved in bullying as a perpetrator or target. Meta-analyses find many predictors of becoming a perpetrator or target of bullying (e.g., Guo, 2016). Bullying occurs across demographics, including age, gender, race/ethnicity, socioeconomic status, and geographic locations. Given the multitude and complexity of factors involved, it is not surprising that prescribed antibullying programs that are meant to eradicate bullying behaviors are only moderately effective (Jiménez-Barbero et al., 2016), suggesting the limitations of a one-size-fits-all way of understanding bullying. Rather, we suggest that individual pathways as well as broader contexts are important to consider in understanding youth involvement with bullying.

2.1 Social-Ecological Theory

Social ecological theory has provided a guiding framework for understanding bullying among individuals through this type of conceptualization, as it takes into consideration multiple factors that play a role in one's life (Benbenishty & Astor, 2005; Bronfenbrenner, 1977). The theory posits that youth behaviors are influenced by individual characteristics as well as factors from a range of nested contextual systems with which the individual interacts. *Microsystems* are those that directly affect youths, such as schools, peer groups, and families, from which they learn behaviors and adopt attitudes and beliefs shared by their peers and families. *Mesosystems* comprise interrelations among these microsystems. For instance, a child's continued involvement with a bullying peer group may be influenced by the manner with which their family respond to such peers and behaviors. The *exosystem* encompasses more distal levels of social ecology, which consists of links between systems that indirectly affect youth (e.g., between what occurs at a parent's work and how this influences their interactions with the child at home), and *macrosystem*, which reflects cultural and societal values. Finally, the *chronosystem* captures changes that occur over time, such as a family moving or parents divorcing, or changes that impact a wide number of people, such as a war or pandemic. Applied to bullying, factors at multiple levels of the social ecology can heighten or reduce risk of victimization – including neighborhood, culture, school organizational, and student factors (Benbenishty & Astor, 2005).

2.2 Social Learning Theory

Children are constantly absorbing, and learning about, what is occurring around them. If a student is having a hard time with her schoolwork, do peers come around to help or do they tease the student? If someone's appearance or personality stands out as different, is he put down as strange or embraced as unique? There are infinite situations in which a child can learn about the dynamics of their social environment via observation of what plays out around them, and this learning, in turn, can contribute to one's own beliefs, attitudes, and behavior.

Children may not only be influenced by observing bullying actions but also by noting the repercussions that follow those actions

According to social learning theory (Bandura, 1986), it is not only the behavior that is observed that can lead to the mimicking of a behavior; the observed consequences of the behavior are also crucial in determining whether or not a behavior will be emulated. Whenever a behavior is enacted, the observer will look for cues that imply whether or not the observed behavior is accepted and rewarded, or not accepted and punished (or at least not rewarded). For example, when a peer is seen getting a lot of positive attention for being a "class clown," the observing child may infer that acting inappropriately (i.e., as the class clown) leads to positive attention from others and will not be punished. The observer will, in turn, be more inclined to enact the behavior because it appears to be beneficial to do so – that is, they will predict that by acting like a class clown they will also receive positive attention. When children observe bullying behaviors they notice how others react, which can be used as evidence for how others may respond to them if they bully others. If the bullying is reinforced with attention and not punished, the child may internalize (i.e., learn) the idea that aggressive bullying behavior is both acceptable (i.e., not punished) and worthwhile (i.e., rewarded) (Bussey & Bandura, 1999).

This type of observational learning also happens outside of school. We know that children are exposed to many different people (models) in their life across various contexts ranging from family members, peers, community members, and others in the broader culture (e.g., media figures). Therefore, children are vulnerable to a wide range of social models from which behavior can be observed and emulated based upon the messages they receive as to whether onlookers respond with positive or negative attention. We will explore several potential social models. starting with peers.

Peer influence is strongly associated with bullying behavior (Cook et al., 2010), and a child may learn to view bullying as acceptable when they observe aggressive and hurtful behavior being reinforced by others. For instance, peers who witness bullying (i.e., as bystanders) may not intervene, or may even encourage the bully (e.g., by laughing, provoking), which can influence the child to *learn* that bullying has only positive consequences and no negative consequences. This notion has been supported by research suggesting that bullying may be more prevalent in school environments in which bystanders reinforce bullying behaviors (e.g., Kärnä et al., 2011). Additionally, children who affiliate with aggressive peers, who may be more likely to positively reinforce bullying, are more likely to enact bullying behavior (Mouttapa et al., 2004). Bullying more often occurs in classrooms that minimize the potential harm of bullying (Pozzoli et al., 2012), which can send the message that bullying is acceptable.

There are many ways that youths can observe bullying behavior being reinforced by others. For one, children may view bullying as a way of building or maintaining popularity. Peers recognize this connection too, and therefore some may seek to mimic that pathway to popularity via bullying. For adolescents, bullying may not increase popularity because those who bully are already popular; rather, they may use bullying as a way to maintain their status (Pouwels et al., 2018). Thus, onlookers may recognize that bullying others is a way to maintain their social status. Overall, children and adolescents recognize the positive association between bullying and social status, and therefore emulate the bully behaviors as a way to reap the expected rewards of social status.

Children who enact hurtful behavior towards others may learn that bullying is tolerated based upon how the targeted peer responds to the bullying behavior. For instance, the targeted individual who struggles to stop the hurtful behavior may end up in a state of learned helplessness. The targeted child may doubt that the hurtful behavior will ever end because their efforts lack any tangible influence, which may lead to a decrease in efforts to resist or stop the bullying. This predicament may explain why meta-analyses have found that being targeted by bullying is relatively stable over time (Kljakovic & Hunt, 2016) and that peer victimization is moderately stable over the course of a year, particularly when there is no intervention to stop it (Pouwels et al., 2016). As such, a futile response from the targeted individual can be interpreted by onlookers as a signal that bullying will be tolerated and there will not be repercussions. In fact, emotional problems (e.g., a depressed state) *and* decreased social status that can emerge from being bullied actually put an individual at risk for being further bullied (Reijntjes et al., 2010). Thus, the negative emotional state and weakened social ties of those who are bullied may make them appear incapable of defending themselves, which can suggest to the onlooker that bullying will not be resisted.

Without intervention, many victims continue to be bullied over time

Another way in which observed bullying can come across as acceptable is when school staff are not vigilant enough to notice and intervene when bullying is occurring. Essentially, with a lack of school staff intervention, onlookers may infer that it is easy to "get away with" bullying, and that there will be no negative consequences. This situation may explain why perceptions of adult monitoring are an important factor in bullying (Wienke Totura et al., 2009). Similarly, positive student–teacher relationships are associated with bystanders standing up to bullying (Thornberg et al., 2017), which again indicates that children look to adults as models when ascertaining whether bullying is an acceptable behavior or not.

Children can also learn by observing social models outside of school, such as within their family. In the case of domestic violence, children can observe that their aggressive parent holds a lot of power within the family. This observation could lead the child to infer that aggression leads to power, and that power is a desirable reward or method to get one's way. Children may also observe aggression as a means to putting an end to interpersonal issues and disputes, which is a dynamic that can also be emulated. In fact, children who bully others are more likely to witness hostile relationships between family members (Connolly & O'Moore, 2003; Espelage et al., 2000), including exposure to familial domestic violence (Bowes et al., 2009). The same pattern of social learning may emerge when children are exposed to social models outside their home. For instance, being surrounded by violence in one's community increases the risk for bullying behavior in school (Espelage et al., 2000).

2.3 Group Dynamics

> Group dynamics, such as favoring in-group members and targeting out-group members, contribute to bullying interactions among youth

Group socialization theory suggests that whenever multiple individuals form a group they will be inclined to adopt favorable attitudes toward their own group and negative attitudes toward other groups (Harris, 2009), which naturally fosters a sense of group identity. A natural consequence of group identity is conformity within the group, which emerges over time. That is, individuals gradually embody the norms of the group (e.g., attitudes, behavioral patterns) and put down individuals who express divergent views or behaviors (Berger & Rodkin, 2012). How might group conformity contribute to bullying? If a child is seeking group identity, and the norms within one's peer group embody behavior that is aggressive or hurtful, it is reasonable to expect that a child may try to maintain group identity by enacting bullying behaviors. Furthermore, individuals who exist within a larger group can feel a sense of anonymity, which can influence one's behavior. Group anonymity may make it easier to enact harmful bullying behaviors with less inhibition because the child may feel like his behavior is blending in with a larger group's behavior (Hirsh et al., 2011), thereby reducing a sense of responsibility and increasing a sense of "oneness" with their group.

> Bullying may occur to exert influence over others or to maintain an established social hierarchy

As previously noted, individuals who already have social power may also bully others simply as a way to *maintain* their power, and not lose it to others. Essentially, children may bully their targets as a way to simply maintain their social dominance and power that they already have and prevent others from taking their power from them, since losing social power can feel threatening and can lead to a loss of resources they acquire from being in power. This notion is based on behavioral ecological theory (Pellegrini, 2008). Similarly, children within peer groups who struggle to manage the complex dynamics and challenges of relationships may resort to bullying rather than more mature mechanisms. This idea has been supported by a recent meta-analysis that showed that social problems were predictive of bullying behavior that the authors hypothesized were influenced by social immaturity (Kljakovic & Hunt, 2016).

As an example, let's say that the desired outcome of a very popular adolescent girl (Mary) is to have a romantic relationship with a particular peer (Mark). Mary may feel threatened by Jane, a less popular girl in their group who happens to be friends with Mark, because Mary does not want anyone else to date him. Imagine that Jane begins gaining popularity within the group, making her appear more desirable to Mark. In this case, Mary, the more popular girl, may bully Jane, the less popular peer, as a way to maintain her social power within the group by making Jane appear less desirable by decreasing her popularity and increasing her own appearance of popularity; thereby increasing her chances of dating Mark. As seen in this example, children may bully peers in their group as a way to maintain their social power, particularly if they feel it is being threatened, in order to ultimately obtain a desired outcome. Individuals who hold a sense of power within their group may feel threatened when their power appears to be vulnerable, and therefore bully others simply as a way to maintain their power and ultimately achieve desired outcomes that they perceive would come with having power.

2.4 Cognitive Factors

As social learning theory explains, children can observe others who bully gain positive consequences and/or not experience negative consequences, which can lead the individual to emulate the bullying. It is important to note, however, that according to social learning theory, children who observe bullying may not necessarily take on the belief that bullying is acceptable and worthwhile; therefore, observing bullying may not lead them to enact bullying themselves. As such, the progression from an individual observing someone bullying another, to the individual doing the bullying themselves, depends on the child's perception and interpretation of the bullying they are observing. Social cognitive learning theory suggests that cognitive factors, such as beliefs and attitudes, determine whether an observed behavior will ultimately become emulated or not (Bandura, 1986). Individuals who observe bullying can adopt biased ways of thinking that justify bullying and thus make it seem acceptable and worthwhile, a concept known as moral disengagement (Gini, 2006). Moral disengagement is particularly related to cyberbullying perpetration (Chen et al., 2017) and aggressive behavior, regardless of gender (Gini et al., 2014).

For some, but not all, children, observing bullying may influence them to engage in bullying

One way individuals can enact moral disengagement is by restructuring their thoughts in a way that makes a behavior appear to be more positive than the behavior seems to be on the surface. Individuals may justify bullying behavior by suggesting that it serves some important purpose that negates the harm that bullying may inflict (Pozzoli et al., 2012). In some cases, a child may justify his or her bullying as a way to give critical feedback to peers, such as when the targeted peer's behavior or quality is disliked or devalued. For instance, imagine a student who is hyperactive and tends to annoy his peers. Those who bully this child may justify that their bullying is necessary because the targeted peer "has it coming to him" or because "they're so annoying" and "needs someone to teach them a lesson."

Children who bully may also downplay the hurt they have inflicted on others by comparing what they have done against more severe behaviors. For instance, a child who verbally bullies a peer may say, "At least I didn't fight them and beat them up. I'm going easy on them, it's just teasing." Additionally, children may use light euphemisms when describing the bullying behavior. One may say, "I'm just messing around with them and ruffling their feathers," even when the behavior is much more hurtful and, in fact, bullying. Children may also justify bullying by declaring that the target of bullying needs to "toughen up" and not be so affected or hurt by the bullying behaviors. This type of justification may emerge when the child doing the bullying is insensitive to the emotional pain felt by their target. In fact, some research suggests that aggressive children may not recognize the emotional states of others (Jolliffe & Farrington, 2011) and therefore dismiss the negative impact their bullying has on their target, which could make bullying seem acceptable in their mind. Additionally, some children who bully may not recognize how their targets feel or do not register the negative consequences of their behavior. For example, children who bully have lower levels of empathy in terms of understanding the thoughts (cognitive empathy) and feelings (affective empathy) of others (Mitsopoulou & Giovazolias, 2015). Further, a lack of negative consequences that follow bullying (i.e., not seeing the hurtful impact) can reinforce the bullying behavior because it can seem innocuous. Alternatively, higher levels of empathy may play a role in bullying for some individuals. That is, the ability to recognize the thoughts and emotions of others can actually be used as a 'tool' for bullying. For example, a student might find vulnerabilities within a peer and exploit them via bullying, and rewards that come from bullying, such as making others laugh or feeling powerful or accepted, become more salient than any feelings of empathy.

What about children who have negative views about bullying behavior and still end up bullying others? Cognitive dissonance theory has been used to explain this phenomenon (Festinger, 1957). According to this theory, although an individual may hold beliefs and values about what is and is not acceptable (e.g., bullying), their behavior is not always in line with their beliefs or values. When this discrepancy occurs, internal distress is experienced because people strive for consistency between their beliefs/values and actions. Cognitive dissonance theory suggests that people resolve this internal distress by changing their beliefs/values so they are more in line with their behavior.

In relation to bullying, cognitive dissonance theory can explain how youths with antibullying attitudes end up in a pattern of bullying. For instance, recall from the section on group dynamics that a child may mimic group norms because "everyone else is doing it." If that child previously held antibullying views, he or she may experience cognitive dissonance. In an effort to relieve that dissonance, the child may gradually shift his or her belief/value from, for instance, "People should *always* treat others with respect and *never* bully others," to "Everyone should strive to treat everyone with respect; however, it is *impossible* to *always* be respectful and sometimes bullying is okay." This change in belief creates room or space within a child's mental structure for previous bullying behavior to exist without dissonance. When the bullying behavior continues over time, one's alterations in beliefs can gradually become extreme to the point that bullying becomes completely acceptable. This may explain why children who play violent/aggressive video games, in which they aggress toward pretend others within a "virtual" world, become increasingly desensitized (and respond with less emotion) to violence/aggression, even when violence could have been something they were previously averse to or found uncomfortable (Calvert et al., 2017).

Bystanders and onlookers to bullying may also play a role in one's justification of bullying. Bystanders may be more or less inclined to intervene or take action when it comes to preventing bullying depending on their own thought processes. Bystanders may be wary of intervening due to fear of being bullied themselves or they may be concerned about losing their social status by standing up to someone who has power (Forsberg et al., 2018). Essentially, bystanders may feel they have something to lose by intervening to stop bullying. In fact, bystanders are less likely to intervene when they are more popular (Sainio et al., 2011). Bystanders may also have a low degree of social self-efficacy (i.e., the belief that one is socially competent and effective), which can prevent them from stepping in to stop bullying (Thornberg & Jungert, 2013) because they may fear they will make a fool of themselves or generally be ineffective in their attempts.

Thought processes of bystanders may influence their decision to intervene or not when observing bullying

Children may also be more likely to justify observed bullying and less likely to intervene when they do not recognize the moral transgression of bullying and its impact on the target (Thornberg & Jungert, 2013). For example, bystanders may interpret bullying as a necessary and/or acceptable behavior in certain circumstances, which is linked with lower levels of intervening (Thornberg & Jungert, 2013). All this being said, there are many reasons why bystanders may not intervene, and therefore the child doing the bullying may justify it by highlighting the lack of negative consequences (i.e., nobody is stopping them).

2.5 Individual Factors for Bullies

Although not always the case, there may be times when the child who is hurting others is actually hurting himself. A recent review of studies suggested that childhood abuse, neglect, and maladaptive parenting were linked to bullying behavior (Nocentini et al., 2019). There are several theories that may explain the link between abuse and bullying behavior. For instance, according to attachment theory, a child's bond with his caregiver is considered a formative relationship that shapes the child's schema for how relationships with others should be experienced and navigated (Bowlby, 1973; Cassidy & Shaver, 2016). An inability to develop a healthy attachment with a caregiver may influence the way in which a child relates with others in school (for a review see Williford et al., 2016). Insecure parent–child attachments have also been theorized to contribute to aggressive styles of interpreting and reacting to social situations (Cassidy et al., 1996; Raikes & Thompson, 2008).

There is not one path for becoming a bully or victim, rather a number of risk factors have been associated for each of these classifications

There have been other risk-factors postulated regarding the development of bullying that are related to emotion regulation/self-control, personality characteristics, and social relationships. In terms of emotion regulation, students with higher levels of anger directed outward toward others were more likely to bully others (Lovegrove et al., 2012). Additionally, children who bully have been found to report higher levels of neuroticism (Mitsopoulou & Giovazolias, 2015). Such internal distress, including anger and hostility, does not necessarily emerge out of the blue. It may be that such youth are grappling with their own negative experiences, which they take out on others. As an example, an emotionally distressed teenager waiting in line for lunch with pent up frustration following a dispute with a teacher earlier in the day may impatiently and aggressively shove a peer out of the way to take his place in line. Another socially anxious teenager who is unable to regulate his or her emotions may feel extremely insecure and unsettled while in a group setting, which results in an angry outburst toward a peer. These theories have been supported by research demonstrating that youths who are bullied themselves can end up engaging in aggressive behavior towards others (Guo, 2016), and that this relationship can be explained by feelings of hostility (Walters & Espelage, 2018).

Self-control – the ability to inhibit one's impulses and delay gratification – is another individual aspect that has been studied in relation to bullying. Similarly, sensation seeking (e.g., doing risky/dangerous activities; Lovegrove et al., 2012), and higher levels of extraversion and lower levels of conscientiousness (Mitsopoulou & Giovazolias, 2015) have each been linked with bullying behavior. However, contextual factors, including a negative school environment and associating with peers who also bully, may reduce this influence (Moon & Alarid, 2015). This may imply that a combination of low self-control and an environment that does not "contain" one's impulses could increase bullying behaviors.

> **Clinical Vignette 1**
> **Academic Challenges as the Underlying Cause of Bullying Behavior**
>
> Jayden is a 13-year-old boy who has been getting into trouble for being mean to others since he transitioned into middle school. Throughout elementary school he had been considered popular and athletic and never thought of as a "trouble-maker" as he had generally been well-liked by his peers and teachers. In elementary school, Jayden's grades were average. Since starting middle school, however, he has received increasing amounts of critical feedback about his work and performance. Jayden has always had difficulties with reading comprehension and staying organized, but with the less demanding expectations of elementary school he was able to get by and "go under the radar," with teachers not being concerned about him academically. Given his solid grades in elementary school, Jayden's identity was in part built around being a decent student. When teachers began to provide critical feedback in middle school, he brushed it off believing he was doing well enough and because Jayden felt that his social life was going quite well. As the academic rigor and pressure increased, particularly in areas in which he had vulnerabilities, Jayden's grades continued to decline. Consequently, Jayden's teachers began to ask him to work harder and indicated that he was not living up to his academic potential. Jayden, however, felt as though he was working hard, and so he began to feel more and more distressed in the presence of his teachers, especially because he had no experience navigating negative feedback

from them. He became self-conscious in school, so much so that he constantly compared himself to his peers to check and be sure that he was measuring up. This mounting social anxiety turned into irritability around others as Jayden became "on edge" and on the defensive, and he snapped at others whenever he felt that he was being judged. As a self-protective mechanism, he began to pre-emptively judge others before they had the chance to judge him. This manifested as putting his peers down and teasing them. As a result, Jayden began losing friends as his peers began to distance themselves from him. Another stressor in Jayden's life was that his parents were having conflicts, making him feel less comfortable at home. Jayden has never really shared his negative emotions or problems with others, not even his parents, and so the problems he was having with schoolwork and his self-esteem were locked up inside Jayden – nobody else knew what was going on in his head. Jayden had become like a different person and nobody could understand why he was acting so negatively and mean to others.

In this vignette, it is evident how Jayden's academic challenges, that had gone under the radar for so long, came to the forefront in middle school, leaving him feeling vulnerable and anxious. It was an identity crisis of sorts, given that he had never had issues in elementary school and had never received critical feedback. Jayden's negative self-image and self-protective mechanisms turned into a downward spiral where bullying others was a way to make himself feel better about himself. However, the core issues of Jayden's bullying behavior (his academic challenges and resulting feelings of vulnerability) were not addressed because these factors were not recognized and due to the fact that Jayden had not opened up his issues. All the while, Jayden's bullying behavior was highlighted as the problem and got all of the attention instead of the underlying issues that were causing his behavior.

2.6 Individual Factors for Victims

Individual characteristics are also associated with being victims of bullying, particularly when they reflect a notable difference that makes one "stand out" from the crowd (e.g., youths with physical illnesses or disabilities; Pinquart, 2017). Additionally, children who present as vulnerable, timid, and anxious are more likely to be bullied (Crawford & Manassis, 2011; Veenstra et al., 2007). It is difficult to disentangle whether children who are bullied end up having these emotional and social problems because they were bullied and/or if they are targeted by bullying because of their emotional and social problems (i.e., they are an "easy target"). Although having internalizing problems and social problems predicted being targeted by bullying at a later time (Kljakovic & Hunt, 2016), it is also likely that experiencing bullying serves to exacerbate these difficulties.

Just as prior abuse may foster the pathway to bullying behavior, a history of previous abuse may contribute to being perpetually targeted by bullying; i.e., being victimized in one form increases the risk of being victimized again later in life (Kljakovic & Hunt, 2016). As an example, parental abuse and neglect and maladaptive parenting have been linked with bullying others and being targeted by bullying (Lereya et al., 2013; Nocentini et al., 2019). One consideration for this abuse-bullying connection is that the abusive experiences may make children more emotionally and behaviorally vulnerable and dysregulated, and therefore an easier target for bullying. Children who have been abused often experience anxiety, depression, and externalizing problems (Evans et al., 2008) and these factors also predict being targeted by bullying (Kljakovic & Hunt, 2016). Children who experience abuse may also have an underdeveloped sense of trust that adults will look out for them, which some suggest may prevent them from help-seeking (Williford et al., 2016). In the case of bullying, this conundrum may prevent those who are victimized by peers from accessing support from others (Kljakovic & Hunt, 2016).

2.7 Theories Specifically Focused on Cyberbullying

Cyberbullying's unique aspects include greater anonymity, larger audiences, and permanence of content

Cyberbullying occurs within a unique context and thus theories that explain traditional bullying cannot necessarily be applied to cyberbullying (Barlett, 2017). First, power dynamics may vary between the "real" and "virtual" world. In a school setting a particular child might lack power, whereas in the online context this same child might yield power in the anonymity the online context offers, and in the ability to reach a large audience. Second, children are more likely to bully others and to be targeted by bullying online than they are to engage in bullying in person (Aboujaoude et al., 2015). Third, given the salience of social media and technology, youths "would rather tolerate negative effects than be disconnected" (Aboujaoude et al., 2015, p. 15). As such, children might be particularly susceptible to be involved in bullying online.

Cyberbullying can happen to anyone at any given moment, and oftentimes from private settings. That is, unlike bullying in a school setting where other peers or adults may be present and able to intervene, cyberbullying is most likely to occur without any observers or bystanders present. Children can instantaneously take out their grievances and negative feelings towards peers with a click of a button on an online platform from which the target cannot avoid or stop (Kowalski et al., 2012). The internet also has a timeless quality, meaning that an experience of being bullied online can last as long as the online content used to bully is available to be seen by others or someone has taken a screenshot of the content. This enduring quality is in contrast to in-person bullying, in which a single experience of being bullied is more or less over once the targeted child escapes the situation.

Another risk factor for cyberbullying is the perception that one has the ability to hide behind the veil of anonymity. For example, perceived anonymity corresponded with more cyberbullying, particularly when procyberbullying attitudes increased (Barlett et al., 2016). If someone feels like they will not be identified as an aggressor – and therefore less likely to suffer consequences such as retaliation, punishment, or even a perception from others that they are "mean-spirited" – they are more likely accept and engage in cyberbullying. Children are less inhibited when they feel anonymous, so an online community in which aggressive behavior is celebrated or accepted may cue an individual to follow those social norms and bully others. Moreover, the lack of interpersonal contact with the targeted individual may increase their disinhibited aggressive behavior (Lapidot-Lefler & Barak, 2012).

2.8 Summary

Bullying is a complex phenomenon with no single factor predictive of a youth's involvement in bullying (as a perpetrator, target, or both). Several theories explain the emergence and maintenance of bullying, including social-ecological and social learning theories. Group dynamics and cognitive factors are also relevant to understanding bullying. Several individual factors are correlated with the likelihood of perpetrating or being victimized by bullying (e.g., being viewed as weak or lacking power, a history of abuse, limited self-regulation skills); critically, these factors must be considered in light of the multiple contexts in which youth are embedded. Finally, although cyberbullying shares some characteristics with in-person bullying (e.g., social norms), its unique features such as anonymity and constant opportunity are important to take into account when considering prevention program elements.

3

Diagnosis and Treatment Indicators

3.1 Assessment of Bullying Experiences

Evaluations of bullying experiences typically assess the extent to which individuals have engaged in bullying behaviors and/or have been targeted by bullying behaviors. Assessments also might evaluate information on the context of bullying (e.g., where bullying typically occurs) or school climate related to bullying (e.g., Williams & Guerra, 2007). A variety of assessment methods have been developed for evaluating bullying experiences (e.g., Hamburger et al., 2011). Some measures are designed to assess typically occurring bullying behaviors (e.g., Crick & Grotpeter, 1995), whereas others are focused on acts committed in a recent specific time period (e.g., past week or past month). Additionally, there are wide-spanning school climate surveys that include assessment of bullying experiences. Interviews are sometimes used to gather information about bullying experiences; however, survey measures have been the predominant assessment approach utilized by researchers, practitioners, and school personnel. Most of the psychometrically validated survey measures available were designed to be completed by the child or adolescent, although a handful of teacher or parent completed measures are also available (see Appendix 2), which are primarily designed for late childhood/early adolescent aged youth. Overall, the selection of measures used to evaluate bullying experiences will typically be informed by the specific areas needing evaluation, the timeframe under consideration, measurement type, and the target population being assessed.

Time frames of interest, measurement type, and target population demographics should guide evaluation decisions

Although there is no diagnostic label for children who bully or are bullied, there is a section of the DSM-5 dedicated to other conditions that may be a focus of clinical attention, which includes V62.4 (Z60.4) social exclusion or rejection (APA, 2013). This section could be used as a diagnostic indicator of bullying victimization. Of course, any comorbidities/correlates of bullying or victimization (e.g., substance use, depression) may be diagnosed and coded as well.

3.1.1 Self-Report Survey Assessments of Bullying and Victimization Experiences

Several self-report, survey format questionnaires are available for assessing bullying experiences. Survey measures of victimization experiences are typically designed for youth aged 8 and older. These measures vary with regard to such aspects as length, item format (e.g., frequency or Likert scale), and timeline specified (e.g., in the past week vs. past school year). In addition, they range from broad evaluations of feeling teased and/or bullied (e.g., peer victimization scale; Austin & Joseph, 1996) to measures of victimization in specific domains (e.g., weight-based teasing scale; Eisenberg et al., 2003) to those that pertain to past experiences (e.g., retrospective bullying questionnaire; Schäfer et al., 2004). Some measures assess both perpetration and victimization experiences, whereas others solely evaluate bullying/aggression against others or solely assess experiences of being targeted by bullying. In addition, several surveys have been designed to assess specific aspects of bullying experiences, such as perceived reasons for bullying and those involved in bullying. Although the majority of measures evaluate in-person bullying experiences, some measures assess specific forms of bullying such as cyber/online experiences (Patchin & Hinduja, 2015) and others measure sexual harassment by peers, which at times is considered under the broad category of bullying (e.g., see the AAUW's *Crossing the Line* report in Hill & Holly, 2011)

> **Self-report measures can efficiently gather information from large numbers of students, who may also be more willing to respond on paper vs. in an interview**

Self-report measures have several strengths; for example, they are often efficient assessments that can be administered to a large group of students in a short period of time. In this way they can be used to evaluate individual or school-wide levels of bullying, and to track student' experiences and potential changes in experiences, over time. Further, surveys may result in more accurate responding given youth can be reluctant to openly discuss bullying experiences (e.g., due to suspected consequences or embarrassment) and may feel more comfortable reporting experiences in a self-report survey. Some of the longer measures (e.g., bully survey; Swearer & Cary, 2003) can also gather detailed information that is similar to what might be generated in an interview. Several self-report scales are described below to illustrate the types of scales available in this domain.

The **Multidimensional Peer Victimization Scale** (Mynard & Joseph, 2000) has 16 items that measure different types of peer victimization in terms of negative physical actions (e.g., punched me), negative verbal actions (e.g., swore at me), social manipulation (e.g., tried to make my friends turn against me), and attacks on property (e.g., tried to break something of mine). Items on this measure are rated in terms of frequency of occurrence (not at all, once, more than once) in the past school year.

The **Peer Experiences Questionnaire** (Vernberg et al., 1999) is a 17-item questionnaire that includes items assessing victimization (overt, relational, general) over the past 3 months, as well as items evaluating student perceptions of whether aggression and victimization of peers is a legitimate and warranted action (i.e., is justified). Each item is rated on a 5-point Likert scale, with separate versions used with 7th–12th grade and elementary school-aged children.

The **Reynolds Bullying Victimization Scales for Schools** (Reynolds, 2003) is a set of three self-report measures designed for use in school or clinical settings. (1) The Bully Victimization Scale (46 items) assesses the enactment of bullying behaviors and being victimized (i.e., overt and relational) in or near school settings over the past month; (2) The Bully Victimization Distress Scale (35 items) assesses students' psychological distress related to being bullied in the past month; (3) The School Violence Anxiety Scale (29 items) assesses anxiety related to potential violence based on feelings about overt peer aggression, relational aggression, and being unsafe in school. Each scale is rated on a 4-point Likert scale, takes approximately 10 minutes to complete, and can be used with children in 3rd–12th grade.

The **Bully Survey – Student Version** (Swearer & Cary, 2003) is a self-report questionnaire that is divided into three sections for assessment of victim, bystander, and bully behaviors. Each section is preceded by a "yes"/"no" screening question to determine if the child has been bullied, seen another child be bullied, or been a bully to others. If the child responds negatively, they asked to move on to the next section. If the child responds affirmatively to a screener question, they are asked to continue answering more specific questions within that section. Additional questions pertain to where and how the bullying occurred, who bullied them or who they bullied most often, how the bullying affected them, why they think the bullying occurred, and who was aware of the problem. Finally, all children are asked to complete a fourth section that assesses general attitudes towards bullying behaviors. Classification of each child's bully status can be made upon completion of this measure (i.e., bully-only, victim-only, bully-victim, or not-involved). This measure was designed for use with children in 3rd–12th grade and takes approximately 10–15 minutes to complete.

The **Illinois Bully Scale** (Espelage & Holt, 2001) is a self-report measure that assesses bullying perpetration (9 items), bullying victimization (4 items), and fighting (5 items). For all items, students are asked to indicate how often they engaged in each activity or how often the experiences happened to them in the last 30 days. Sample items include: "I upset other students for the fun of it," "Other students called me names," and "I got into a physical fight." Response options range from $0 = $ *never* to $4 = $ *7 or more times*. Scores for each subscale are computed by summing respective items. The scale has demonstrated adequate validity and reliability (Espelage & Holt, 2001). Notably, the scale has been expanded for some evaluations, for instance in an evaluation of Second Step, an evidence-based school bullying prevention program, to capture a wider range of bullying victimization items (Espelage, Low, Van Ryzin et al., 2015).

3.1.2 Others' Reports of Bullying and Victimization Experiences

Peer nomination methods have been used in various studies of peer experiences (e.g., friendship, social support, classroom dynamics), and have also been applied to assessments of bullying and victimization. The peer nomination approach typically involves youth specifying individuals they believe are involved in bullying based upon what they have observed (e.g., observations of peers' behaviors in the classroom). For example, this method can involve asking youth to list same-gender classmates who they perceive as similar to narrative examples provided that reflect bullying (e.g., "This boy, Oscar, is picked on, made fun of…"; Gotthiel & Dubow, 2001), with two of the narratives describing youth who engage in bullying behaviors and two narratives describing youth who are victims of bullying (one example each for boys and girls). The **Modified Peer Nomination Inventory** asks youth to list same-sex peers that they believe fit with items on a list of more concise descriptors (e.g.,

Peer nominations, which involve asking youth to rate or rank peers on specific behaviors can also be used for evaluating bullying or school/class climate

"kids do mean things to him/her"; Perry et al., 1988) and includes indicators of both victimization and bullying behaviors (7 items for each). An alternative approach involves children rating each classmate (as *never*, *sometimes*, or *often*) on a list of concise bullying-related behaviors to determine different roles assumed by students (e.g., bully, assistant, reinforcer, defender, outsider; Salmivalli & Voeten, 2004).

The **Child Social Behavior Questionnaire** uses peer nomination to assess for students involved in bullying-like behaviors either as the victim (e.g., "Being picked on by another child in your class") or perpetrator (e.g., "Breaking another child's things because s/he wanted to upset them?" (Warden et al., 2003). There is also a teacher version that can be used to measure the extent to which a specific student is a victim of bullying or enacts bullying behaviors toward others (e.g., "psychologically hurting another child in class") (Warden et al., 2003).

> Parents, teachers, school counselors, and other adults should be involved to provide additional perspectives in assessments of bullying

Counselors can be interviewed to help confirm the identification of bullies and victims through peer nomination (Phillips & Cornell, 2012). Given that mental health issues are prevalent among bullies *and* victims (e.g., Holt et al., 2015), counselors are likely to be involved in working with these students and therefore privy to knowing which students are involved in bullying. There are not presently counselor specific report surveys for bullying, although counselors can utilize interviewing (see Section 3.1.4: Interviews) and methods similar to peer nomination. Parents may not be reliable reporters when it comes to their awareness of those who are involved in bullying (e.g., Holt et al., 2009), likely because they are not typically present when bullying occurs. Nonetheless, parents may report bullying behaviors on measures that assess a wide range of behaviors, such as the **Child Behavior Checklist** (Achenbach & Rescorla, 2001).

3.1.3 Observations

Bullying and victimization can also be assessed in real-time via observation. The benefit of utilizing observational methods to assess bullying is that they can be implemented in settings where bullying often occurs and yet does not typically have a high degree of school staff oversight, such as on the playground, during recess, and in the cafeteria. A variety of staff can make the observation (e.g., counselors, teachers, assistants), which has the added benefit of utilizing all resources in times when scheduling can be difficult. The use of observation may also cut costs for schools in comparison to purchasing copyrighted measures. One limitation of observation is that it provides a mere snapshot of a student's entire school experience, and so it is possible for conclusions to be made that do not reflect the student's broader experiences in school. Despite these concerns, children at play tend to lose their sense of being watched, particularly if adults are observing over extended periods of time and in inconspicuous areas. Observations are an effective way to collect separate data that can be used to confirm or disprove other sources of data (e.g., interview, surveys), and may inform where intervention most needs to occur. Although less common, it is important to note that some researchers have used video cameras to capture and code bullying behaviors, along with teacher and student interventions and reinforcement of bullying behaviors (e.g., Craig et al., 2000).

3.1.4. Interviews

Interviewing is a helpful way to gather nuanced information about children involved in bullying. Interviewers should use an exploratory and nonjudgmental approach, to reduce defensiveness, and best understand the experiences of all those involved. Interviews can provide rich data; however, unfortunately there are no validated structured interview protocols specific to bullying. There are clinical diagnostic interviews that can be used in a modular fashion, meaning that particular components can be utilized. For instance, since bullying is often associated with depressive symptoms, a counselor may use questions from a depression module and segue into follow-up questions that ask about bullying experiences. Alternatively, an unstructured interview, for example guided by a counselor, can be conducted with individuals involved in bullying to determine relevant details.

Utilizing Functional Behavior Assessment, an assessment tool that does not only identify the presence of a behavior but also helps to understand how the behavior functions within a particular context (Slattery, 2019), can also be an important part of conducting interviews and observations. Functional Behavior Assessment is a way to uncover the antecedents, or contextual factors like setting and circumstances, that precede the bullying behavior, as well as the consequences that follow the bullying behavior in order to understand what is reinforcing the bullying. Consequences can include positive reinforcement, which may involve a student bullying others as a way to get attention. Consequences can also include negative reinforcement, such as a student bullying others to relieve her own feelings of insecurity in social settings or perhaps the pain from maltreatment she is experiencing in other settings. Honing in on the antecedents and consequences allows one to target interventions in a more effective manner by changing the reinforcement patterns (e.g., helping the child find other ways to get attention, feel more secure and less emotional pain).

Functional behavioral assessments can be used to identify antecedents and consequences that perpetuate bullying patterns

Identifying the ways in which bullying is perpetuated within the bully–victim relationship can also guide interventions. A counselor or other staff can gain information from those involved (bully, victim, bystanders, adults, staff) to learn more about the dynamics that may be reinforcing the bullying. For example, knowing the way in which bystanders react and respond to bullying can be very helpful and discovered by interviewing all those who are involved in bullying incidents. Perhaps youth (and even adults) are too afraid to speak up even though they do not like the bullying; or, they may not realize the impact the bullying is having, in which case bystander intervention may be warranted.

Interviewing can also reveal aspects of the victim that can be maintaining the bullying and therefore be a target for intervention. Perhaps the victim is alone while the bullying is happening, does not have any way of standing up for himself, is feeling a low sense of self-esteem, and/or would benefit from assertiveness training or guidance to bolster his social support (Salmivalli, 1999) and seek allies in peers or adults. Interviewing may also reveal that the victim lacks a sense of confidence to stand up to bullies because he is not utilizing his strengths or he may be put in roles in which he could thrive and feel good about himself. He may also lack self-awareness of social behaviors that might provoke bullying from others, such as invading personal space or privacy, "trying too hard" to fit in, making immature jokes, being pushy, "bossy," or a "know it all," or any behavior considered off-putting or "annoying." In this case, the child may benefit from coaching to adjust his social behavior, so long as doing so would be aligned with his own personal values and goals and not simply forced as a way to 'mold' the person for the sake of conformity. Sometimes children simply would benefit from finding different friends if they struggle to "click" with a particular group that ends up bullying them. Children sometimes think they *need* to "fit in" with a particular group even if they are not a great "fit" (based on qualities, interests, personality, etc.), and essentially "force" themselves into the group due to their own insecurity about not "fitting in" with the group for one reason or another. Interviewing can help to identify if this is the case.

Victims may also struggle with anxious and passive behaviors that put them at risk for being bullied. This may be related to internal factors like difficulties with emotion regulation, a negative self-concept related to past traumas, or learned helplessness. Family factors may also play a role in maintaining bullying, such as *over*-protective parenting practices in response to their child's anxiety, which can unintentionally instill a vulnerable identity and prevent the child from confidently dealing with challenges (Smokowski & Kopasz, 2005). At the other end of the continuum, parents may not be emotionally supportive enough of their child who is being bullied. On the other side of the bullying, the bully's beliefs about their behavior may also be reinforced by messages that they are internalizing from family members or other adults, like disrespectful behavior being accepted or praised. Just the same, victims' parents may evoke dysregulated, retaliatory aggression and resentment (within themselves as parents, as well as within their child) that might contribute to provocation for continued bullying and further issues.

In summary, it may be helpful to interview those involved in bullying to uncover factors that can contribute to bullying. These include the personal factors, like the reasons a child may be bullying in the first place, as well as interpersonal dynamics that emerge within and between groups. Information that can be gained via interview can be vital to taking a more individualized and contextual approach to stopping bullying. To the extent possible that family-factors are assessed and accessible, parents can be involved in intervention to target such factors. All in all, interviewing is important because bullying can occur in very different ways because each person, and every social group, is unique in their own, subtle ways, and as such, bullying can vary across individuals, time and contexts.

3.2 Assessment of Correlates or Difficulties Commonly Associated With Bullying

To understand the nature of bullying, one must consider the challenges that often accompany those who are involved in bullying. There are risk factors that increase the likelihood of bullying or being bullied, as well as aspects that may reinforce or maintain bullying involvement. There are also issues that may be consequences of bullying involvement. Assessing these many factors helps to inform a conceptualization of each individual involved in bullying, which can in turn inform a targeted and individualized intervention. While there are certainly systemic school-wide aspects that have been assessed and targeted by interventions over the years with a degree of success (e.g., Jiménez-Barbero et al., 2016), there are also individually based factors that can inform ways to intervene on a more personal level.

Bullies and victims are both at risk for experiencing comorbid difficulties that should be addressed as they may play a role in the initiation and maintenance of bullying involvement. For instance, assessing for comorbid internalizing and externalizing disorders, as well as other social and emotional domains that have been linked with bullying and victimization experiences (e.g., social problems, family issues, attribution style, empathy, aggression, social support, problem solving, emotion regulation, interpersonal effectiveness) is important for best understanding the context and various individual and ecological systems variables at play. In fact, a review of the literature suggests that individual- and family-focused interventions that address these personal factors have a slightly stronger impact on reducing bullying, delinquent, and aggressive behavior compared to school-focused interventions that address the school environment, although all were found to be effective (Farrington et al., 2017). The individually focused interventions include programs that support the aggressor, such as anger management, impulse control training, and cognitive behavioral therapy (CBT). The family-focused programs include family-therapy. Both individual- and family-focused interventions reduce aggressive behavior, suggesting that perpetrators of bullying need adults to understand their personal issues as much as their victims do. Additionally, school-wide bullying intervention programs lose effectiveness among older students/adolescents (Yeager et al., 2015), which suggests that assessing individualized factors of those involved in bullying may be a warranted approach for combatting bullying particularly as children get older.

All this being stated, it is important to not only measure the phenomenon of bullying and victimization as it occurs, but to also understand the individuals who are involved in bullying on a personal level. Doing so can provide an added target for intervention beyond school-wide policies and strategies. Addressing the forces that drive a child to bully others may ultimately alter the life course of all those involved as there are potential consequence of bullying that should also be assessed. Knowing this type of information can also assist the counselor and other school staff in addressing the child's need for emotional support, rather than simply punishing them for the bullying behavior.

Survey questionnaires and interviews can be completed by youth or others (e.g., parents) to identify symptoms and problems that co-exist. For example, broad-spectrum structured interviews (e.g., the Schedule for Affective Disorders and Schizophrenia for School Aged Children, Kaufman et al., 2016) and survey questionnaires (e.g., Child Behavior Checklist, Achenbach & Rescorla, 2001; Behavior Assessment System for Children – BASC-3; Reynolds & Kamphaus, 2015) can be used to identify internalizing (e.g., anxiety, depression), social (e.g., isolation) and externalizing (e.g., impulsiv-

> Social, emotional, and behavioral difficulties commonly co-occur with bullying and should be incorporated into intervention plans

ity, oppositionality) problems. Similarly, school-level surveys may be used to understand the collective experience of students on issues of bullying and related behaviors. For example, the Youth Risk Behavior Surveillance System (YRBSS, CDC, 2019) can be used to identify various youth issues such as risk taking behaviors (e.g., substance use, sexual activity), dating violence, and unsafe feelings at school or in the community. Survey measures can also be utilized to assess for strengths and protective factors that may help children to either resist bullying or be resilient despite it. Surveys like the Developmental Assets Profile can be helpful, as they assess a wide range of external assets (e.g., support, empowerment) and internal assets (e.g., social competencies, positive identity; Search Institute, 2016).

In sum, to gain a more comprehensive understanding of any given youth who is involved in bullying it is important to assess a range of correlates, including co-morbid concerns and strengths. This will allow for more tailored and in turn effective interventions to be implemented.

Clinical Vignette 2
Complex Behaviors: Bullies Being Bullied

In this case vignette, pay attention to the elements that would be considered part of bullying in an assessment: intent to harm, repetition, and a power differential.

Raquel is a 17-year-old high school senior. She has been experiencing a lot of issues in her friend group, which led her to be referred for counseling. Raquel disclosed to her counselor that she has a prior history of peer difficulties and has been feeling left out by her friend group for several months now. She explained how her friends make plans but do not invite her and then make up lies to avoid being honest about excluding her.

As a child, Raquel was more interested in activities like playing with action figures, tinkering, and competing in sports. At that time, Raquel had generally been accepted by her male peer group, but as she got older, the boys began to distance themselves from her. The boys teased her for trying to be like them and excluded her from activities in an aggressive way. Her female peers also rejected her, calling her a tomboy, which was very upsetting to her. These experiences made Raquel feel like she did not fit in with anyone and she began to feel angry and resentful, leading her to act irritable and reactive around others, which in turn resulted in her feeling even more isolated and rejected. Eventually she had no friends in elementary school. When starting middle school, Raquel was motivated to make friends. She worked hard to be "perfect" so that she could impress others and be accepted. She got all A's, worked hard in sports to be the best on her team, and did everything she could to go "under the radar" and avoid drama, hoping that people would start to like her. And people did start to respect Raquel and compliment her for being good at things. At some point, she joined a peer group made up of girls where she was not considered popular and kept feeling like an outsider even when she spent time with group members. She was jealous of the more popular girls in her new friendship group and began to stir up drama by spreading rumors about others and speaking badly about her friends behind their backs. At first, Raquel was getting attention from others, being the person others would go to to hear about the drama going on. Raquel's power came in the form of knowing a lot about everyone's personal business and using it against them. In this way she felt like she was holding onto friends, which was reinforcing her behavior. Raquel felt popular and used that power to make herself look good by making others look bad.

Eventually, her friends realized that Raquel was fragmenting the friendship group and retaliated by talking negatively about Raquel for spreading rumors and creating drama. They posted messages on social media telling everyone how "toxic" Raquel was and urging others to stay away from her. Raquel was devastated. In the classroom and on the school premises, members of her former peer group kept calling Raquel toxic and aggressively told her to stay away from them whenever she came near, humiliating Raquel in front of her classmates. Raquel began losing the friendships that she had worked so hard to gain. She doubled down on her own negative behaviors out of fear of looking bad and continued to create drama and spread rumors as a way to make herself look like the "good person" who was being excluded by her friends.

This case illustrates the complexity of the negative behaviors that can be involved in bullying. On the one hand, Raquel could be considered a victim of bullying from her time in elementary school which resulted in her continued feelings of resentfulness and anger. Later in school, Raquel was unkind to members of her peer group by creating drama which in turn made them feel that they were just defending themselves and therefore victims of bullying. Key elements of bullying are present in this case. For instance, the intent to do harm is evident in Raquel's rumor spreading but also in her friends' actions when they retaliated. The harmful behaviors were repeated over time, however, the issue of the power imbalance is more complicated. It could be argued that Raquel's friends held the power since they were popular within the group while Raquel was more of an outsider and newbie joining the group. But Raquel may have also held power when she became more popular due to spreading rumors. Therefore, power may be conceptualized as fluid in this case. In sum, given the complicated dynamics in this constellation, it could be suggested that both Raquel and her peers were engaging in bullying while also being targeted by bullying.

4

Treatment

There are no targeted individual treatments specifically designed for those involved in bullying. Rather, bullying and its potential consequences may be addressed in therapy using a variety of frameworks (e.g., CBT). However, as detailed below there is a substantial body of research on school-based prevention programs aimed to reduce bullying. Please also see Appendix 1 for a list of useful websites, apps, and events.

School-based programs designed to address bullying are most common and effective to scale

4.1 Methods of Treatment

As described in subsequent sections, effective bullying prevention programs involve a whole school approach. These approaches may also include targeted supports for students engaged in bullying perpetration or who have been victimized by bullying, but the overarching goal of such programs is to create a school climate that does not tolerate bullying and in which teachers and students feel they have the skills and confidence to engage in bystander behaviors that reduce any bullying behaviors that do occur.

Bullying prevention programs using a whole school approach have been found to be most effective

4.2 Mechanisms of Action

A core assumption of the majority of bullying prevention programs is that for bullying behaviors within a school to change, all members of the school – from students to teachers to administrators – must have a clear understanding of what bullying behaviors are and a commitment to not tolerating or engaging in such behaviors. Thus, a key mechanism of action for bullying reduction is modifying norms around bullying, which in turn promotes a more positive school climate. There are also program-specific proposed mechanisms for action. The most widely used bullying prevention programs have clearly articulated theories of change, through which the mechanisms of action to reduce bullying are explicated. For instance, some programs address bullying through a broader social-emotional learning framework, whereas other programs (particularly those for adolescents) focus on building effective bystander skills among students. Below we provide information about bullying prevention program efficacy broadly, and then turn to specific programs and their approaches to addressing this issue.

4.3 Efficacy

> **Meta-analyses synthesize the effects of specific interventions or programs across all available studies that meet established quality criteria**

Antibullying legislation now exists in numerous countries and all 50 states in the US, reflecting a positive step forward in addressing bullying. However, only about half of the states explicitly encourage bullying prevention within the legislation, and only 14 states mandate bullying prevention programs in public K–12 schools (Srabstein et al., 2008). Further, among states requiring the implementation of bullying prevention programs, legislation most often does not provide specific recommendations of programs or features of programs nor funding for schools to implement such programs (Srabstein et al., 2008). This makes it challenging for schools to identify optimal programs to implement, particularly if school staff are unaware of national registries that provide this information, such as Blueprints for Healthy Youth Development (https://www.blueprintsprograms.com), and the Office of Juvenile Justice and Delinquency Prevention's Model Programs Guide (https://www.ojjdp.gov/mpg).

Notably, one source of information about programs historically was the National Registry for Evidence-Based Prevention Programs, but this was discontinued in 2018 (Green-Hennessey, 2018). We highlight the National Registry for Evidence-Based Prevention Programs here given some of the programs we describe below had been identified as effective for particular outcomes by them. Further, although there are a number of reviews and meta-analyses of bullying prevention programs, this information is not always effectively disseminated to schools, and therefore at the school-level there is limited knowledge about the state of bullying prevention research more broadly.

In this section, we summarize what is known about the efficacy of bullying prevention programs broadly, and then turn to descriptions of three programs that have demonstrated some evidence of effectiveness. We close with challenges related to effectively implementing evidence-based bullying prevention programs.

Research on the effectiveness of bullying prevention programs has yielded mixed, although promising, findings, as evidenced by systematic reviews and meta-analyses. In one of the first systematic reviews, Vreeman and Carroll (2007) found that effectiveness varied by program type; whole-school approaches were more effective than classroom-based curriculum programs, for instance. This was in contrast to earlier reviews (Ferguson et al., 2007; Smith et al., 2004) which concluded that, for the most part, programs did not result in self-reported declines in bullying victimization and perpetration. Other more recent systematic reviews have also demonstrated promising findings (Evans et al., 2014; Farrington & Ttofi, 2009; Merrell et al., 2008). Based on the 30 programs reviewed by Farrington and Ttofi (2009), findings indicated that, on average, there were reductions of 17–23% for victimization and 20–30% for bullying perpetration. Notably, there were stronger effects in Europe than in the United States. Further, in their 2011 meta-analytic extension of this systematic review, there were significant program effects for victimization and perpetration (Ttofi & Farrington, 2011). Notably, effect sizes were stronger for evaluations of the Olweus Bullying Prevention Program (described in Section 4.4.1) than other programs. Evans and colleagues (2014) extended these findings in their systematic review, which included 32 evaluations of bullying interventions from 2009–2014. This review did not synthesize the extent of reductions in victimization and perpetration, but rather considered how many studies reported statistically significant changes in these outcomes. Significant effects were detected in more cases for victimization (67% of studies) than bullying perpetration (50% of studies). Again, studies documenting significant reductions were more likely to have been conducted outside the United States, which could be due to the greater heterogeneity of the United States on a number of dimensions.

Two recent meta-analyses addressed more specific questions around bullying prevention program efficacy. The first examined differences in efficacy based on youth developmental periods. Specifically, findings from Yeager and colleagues (2015) indicated that for youth up to 7th grade, bullying preventions were effective at reducing bullying, whereas for high school youth there were at times iatrogenic effects (i.e., bullying increased in schools in which prevention programs were implemented). The second meta-analysis assessed the efficacy of programs aimed at increasing bystander interventions. In this case, programs were successful at increasing students' positive bystander behaviors, particularly when implemented in high school settings (Polanin et al., 2012). Taken together, these findings point to the salience of considering the age of the youth population when determining which type of bullying prevention/intervention program to implement.

Studies have revealed differences in bullying prevention program efficacy based on age

4.4 Variations and Combinations of Methods

Next, we turn to descriptions of three of the most widely used and evaluated bullying prevention/intervention programs – the Olweus Bullying Prevention Program, KiVa, and Second Step Social-Emotional Learning – and for each provide information about their effectiveness.

4.4.1 Olweus Bullying Prevention Program (OBPP)

Dan Olweus designed the OBPP as part of a nationwide effort in Norway to reduce school-based victimization, spurred by youth suicides that were in part attributed to bullying. The OBPP is aimed at youth in elementary through middle school (Limber, 2006). The program guide also offers information on adapting the program for high school students, although to date the program has only been evaluated for adolescents through 10th grade.

The OBPP is one of the oldest and most well studied programs in the world

The OBPP is a whole-school, universal, approach with program components at four levels: individual, classroom, school, and community. Given that it is a universal intervention, all students are involved. Students who perpetrate bullying and/or are targeted by bullying also receive additional supports. Program developers stress the importance of school staff spending considerable time planning for program implementation – approximately 4 to 6 months – along with a certified Olweus program trainer. At the individual level, elements include staff responding immediately to bullying incidents, supervision of students' activities; meeting with parents of children involved in bullying, and developing specific intervention plans for students involved in bullying. Regular student meetings, and posting of school rules about bullying, are part of the classroom level intervention. The school level consists of components including the initial program kick-off event, training for staff and teachers, the development of a Bullying Prevention Coordination Committee, and fostering parent involvement. Moreover, the school is expected to administer the Olweus Bullying Questionnaire to determine students' baseline experiences with bullying perpetration and victimization, and repeat the questionnaire following program implementation (typically once per year) to identify any changes that may have occurred. Finally, community involvement is essential, and spans from community members serving on the Bullying Prevention Coordination Committee to schools developing partnerships with community agencies.

There are a range of program materials available. The Bullying Prevention Coordinating Committee uses a schoolwide guide (with a DVD and CD) with detailed information about how to implement the OBPP. For teachers, there is a comprehensive teacher guide (with a DVD and CD), that includes all necessary implementation resources. A questionnaire is another key program component, and as such schools have the option to select scannable questionnaires that are processed by Hazelden Publishing, after which schools are provided with reports. Alternatively, schools can select photocopies of the questionnaire that in turn school staff need to process. Spanish and English versions of the questionnaire are offered.

To date the OBPP has been evaluated primarily in Norway but more recently in the United States as well. The first large-scale evaluation of OBPP involved 2,500 Norwegian students in 5th–8th grade (Olweus, 2005). Youth were followed for 2.5 years, and reductions in both bullying perpetration and victimization were documented across this period. Specifically, in the three cohorts under consideration in this study, percentage reductions in victimization ranged from 4.5–4.9%, and percentage reductions in bullying perpetration ranged from 2.1–2.8%. In addition, improvements were seen in rates of antisocial behaviors, classroom discipline, attitudes toward school, and satisfaction with school life.

A large scale evaluation of the OBPP in the United States started in Pennsylvania in 2007 and was estimated to have reached over 200,000 students by 2012 (The Highmark Foundation, 2009). This reflects approximately 13% of schools and students in Pennsylvania, and through this initiative multiple cohorts were followed (2008, 2009, and 2010). Overall, for elementary, middle, and high school students, reductions in peer victimization occurred following program implementation; decreases varied by cohort. For instance, for the 2008 cohort bullying victimization decreased by 13% for high school youth from 2008–2010, whereas reductions of 5% were seen for the 2009 high school cohort from 2009–2010. With respect to bullying perpetration, bullying perpetration decreased by 6.7% for high school students for the 2007–2009 cohort, and by 2% for the 2008–2009 cohort. Findings that reductions were most pronounced for high school students is in contrast to other research highlighting bullying prevention programs to not be helpful for high school youth (Yeager et al., 2015). Notably, other positive program effects were also found, including more students perceiving that adults in their schools were actively working to stop bullying, and more students indicating that they would intervene if a peer was being bullied.

Findings from this OBPP evaluation were published in 2012, and focused on a sample of approximately 56,000 students and 2,400 teachers over a 2-year period (Schroeder et al., 2012). Key findings from this set of analyses indicated that program participation was associated with reductions in bullying perpetration and victimization, and increases in attitudes against bullying as well as beliefs that adults are responsive to bullying. The most recent set of analyses from the Pennsylvania quasi-experimental study examined program outcomes for students in 3rd–11th grade (Limber et al., 2018). For the majority of grades, findings demonstrated significant reductions in bullying victimization and perpetration. However, for bullying victimization there were not statistically significant changes over time for 8th, 10th, and 11th grade students. For bullying perpetration, there were significant reductions in all grades, with most notable changes for high school youth. Program effects were similar for boys and for girls, but there were differences by race/ethnicity (i.e., program effects were weaker for Black and Hispanic youth).

Recent research has pointed to potential benefits of coupling the OBPP with skill-building components for particular subgroups of students (Sullivan et al., 2017). Specifically, in a study evaluating differences in outcomes between middle school classrooms exposed to the OBPP only and classrooms exposed to the OBPP and lessons from Second Step (described later in this chapter), the researchers found that there were no overall differences between these two intervention approaches. However, findings indicated that youth with disabilities in the combined condition, compared to the OBPP only condition, reported greater improvements in teacher-reported social skills. In addition, students without disabilities in the combined condition reported more anger regulation coping skills. Finally, boys in the combined intervention demonstrated greater decreases in externalizing behaviors and bullying perpetration based on teacher reports than those in the OBPP only condition. Studies such as this one highlight the importance of better understanding differential effects of school-based programs for subgroups (Farrell et al., 2013).

Consistent with the importance of fidelity in program implementation broadly, fidelity affects bullying prevention program effectiveness (Smith et al., 2004). Given that the OBPP is delivered by teachers, a small body of research has also explored the extent to which teacher characteristics affect program implementation and outcomes. In one study focused on middle school students, teacher delivery competence made a significant additional contribution to student responsiveness to the OBPP, beyond that which was explained by instructional behavioral adherence (Goncy et al., 2015).

Finally, emerging evidence from both Sweden and the United States suggests that the Olweus Bullying Prevention Program is a cost effective approach that can result in considerable societal benefits (Beckman & Svensson, 2015). In the United States in particular, cost–benefit analyses based on Pennsylvania data indicated that by reducing high school bullying, the cost benefit to society would be nearly 1.5 million dollars per individual over their lifetime (The Highmark Foundation, 2012).

More information about the Olweus Bullying Prevention Program can be found at https://www.violencepreventionworks.org/public/bullying.page#:~:text=The%20Olweus%20Bullying%20Prevention%20Program,the%20course%20of%20three%20years.

4.4.2 Kiusaamista Vastaan (KiVa)

> KiVa aims to increase antibullying attitudes, defending behaviors, and self-efficacy of bystanders

In Finland, the Ministry of Education mandated the development of an antibullying program to be offered to all schools country-wide (Salmivalli et al., 2011). The result was KiVa (Kiusaamista Vastaan; Finnish for against bullying) – a program that emphasizes the interpersonal dynamics of bullying with a particular focus on the bystander. The overarching goal of KiVa is to change responses to bullying from all individuals in the schools, including teachers and students, which will in turn result in an improved school climate. Although originally targeted at 4th–6th grade students, KiVa now includes 3 units, each of which is based on a specific age range of youth (6–9, 10–12, 13–16). KiVa includes both universal and indicated elements. With respect to program details, at the universal level KiVa involves a 20-hour curriculum that aims to increase antibullying attitudes, defending behaviors, and self-efficacy of bystanders. Program components include role plays, a video game, a film, and the use of discussions and group work. Indicated level activities focus on youths involved in bullying as victims or perpetrators, and can also involve interventions that bolster students' support of victims for students who have encountered difficulties doing so. The KiVa program package also includes online tools for schools to use that result in yearly reports highlighting program outcomes and implementation indicators. For additional details about the KiVa program, please refer to the program's website http://www.kivaprogram.net.

Studies in both Finland and other countries have indicated that KiVa is an effective bullying prevention program. For instance, in a study of 4th–6th grade students, there were significant reductions in bullying and peer victimization in the intervention schools across a 12-month period (Kärnä et al., 2011). Specifically, at Wave 2 (9 months after baseline), peer-reported victimization rates had declined, and at Wave 3 (12 months after baseline) reductions in intervention schools emerged for peer-reported victimization, self-reported victimization, and self-reported bullying perpetration. These findings also held when considering particular forms of bullying (e.g., verbal, physical, cyber); each form decreased in intervention schools, in contrast to control schools in which either bullying increased or decreased significantly less than evident in intervention schools. Promising results were found for other indicators as well, though the effects primarily held only at Wave 2. For instance, at Wave 2 students in the intervention condition were more likely to defend peers who were being bullied, and less likely to assist or reinforce the bully. Similarly, students who had participated in Kiva were more likely to hold antibullying attitudes and have higher levels of empathy at Wave 2 than students in control schools. Researchers considered demographic characteristics – age and sex, specifically – relative to program effects, and found for the most part there were no significant differences. However, for peer-reported bullying at Waves 2 and 3, results indicated that effects were more pronounced for older students.

Using the same sample as described above, Williford and colleagues (2012) reported reductions in internalizing problems (depression and anxiety) and differences in peer-group perceptions in schools that implemented KiVa compared to control schools. Notably, reductions in victimization predicted subsequent changes in anxiety and depression; only for anxiety were there statistically significant differences between intervention and control schools. Articulating pathways between victimization and mental health is essential given the clear link between victimization and internalizing problems discussed earlier in this book. This study provides promising evidence to suggest that students in schools that implement KiVa may not only experience reductions in bullying, but also experience improved mental health. Findings from this study relative to peer perceptions were more complex. Across the course of the study, students in both the intervention and control conditions reported more negative peer perceptions (defined as trustworthiness, kindness, and support from peers). Decreases in peer perceptions were stronger for students in the control vs. intervention condition, however.

Some research on KiVa has explored which particular groups of youth might benefit most from program involvement. Specifically, Juvonen and colleagues (Juvonen et al., 2016) conducted a randomized trial over a 12-month period of 4th–6th grade Finnish students to determine whether secondary prevention effects emerged (i.e., whether victimized students in particular experienced reductions in harm). Results indicated that for perceptions of a caring school climate, the most victimized students at baseline were the students who demonstrated the most benefits in this domain (Juvonen et al., 2016). In this same study, findings indicated that there were particularly striking intervention effects on depression and self-esteem for 6th graders who reported the most victimization at baseline, highlighting key developmental differences. Notably, school attitudes at follow-up did not vary by level of victimization at baseline; rather, all students in the intervention condition reported improved school attitudes compared to students in the control condition.

The majority of research on KiVa focuses on 4th–6th grade youth, given this was the initial population for whom the prevention program was designed, though the limited research findings on younger and older youth suggest demonstrate some promise. Specifically, in an evaluation of Finnish students in grades 2–3 and grades 8–9, self-reported bullying perpetration decreased in intervention schools for students in grades 2–3 (Kärnä et al., 2013). Reductions in self-reported bullying victimization for grade 2–3 students were related to the gender of the student, and the gender composition of the classroom (e.g., at the 1-year follow-up, reductions in victimization occurred for girls in classroom with relatively equal numbers of boys and girls). Self-reported victimization and perpetration did not decrease in intervention schools, relative to control schools, for 8th–9th grade students. However, peer-reported victimization decreased within this group, specifically for younger students within this group.

Although most of the research on KiVa has been conducted in Finland, a handful of studies have been conducted elsewhere including Italy, The Netherlands, and Wales. Collectively results indicate that KiVa is an effective program in multiple countries' contexts. For instance, in a study by Nocentini and Menesini (2016), 13 Italian schools were randomly assigned to intervention and control conditions, and 4th and 6th grade students were assessed over an approximately 8-month period. Rates of bullying and victimization decreased for 4th grade students who participated in KiVa, relative to 4th grade students in control schools, as did attitudes supportive of bullying, and attitudes supportive of victims and empathy increased. Within the 6th grade, bullying victimization and perpetration decreased for those in the intervention condition, as did attitudes supportive of bullying. Effect sizes were stronger for elementary students than middle school students. In addition, in a pilot pre–post study of 9–11-year-old Welsh students, overall results indicated that there were reductions in bullying victimization and perpetration (Hutchings & Clarkson, 2015). When considering findings by sex, these findings held for girls, but for boys only reductions in bullying perpetration were evident.

Haataja and colleagues (2014) analyzed data from a large sample of Finnish elementary school students to examine the extent to which KiVa implementation affects outcomes. When considering findings after 9 months of program implementation, results indicated that two key factors were associated with reductions in bullying victimization: lesson adherence by teachers, and the amount of time teachers devoted to preparing lessons. However, no implementation factors emerged as significantly associated with declines in bullying perpetration.

4.4.3 Second Step Social-Emotional Learning

Suite of programs with developmentally tailored lessons for preschool, elementary, and middle school

Second Step Social-Emotional Learning is a suite of programs designed by the Committee for Children, a nonprofit, global agency located in Seattle, WA, that is focused on social-emotional learning. An overview is provided below; for more information about Second Step, please refer to the program's website at https://www.secondstep.org/second-step-social-emotional-learning.

Second Step Social-Emotional Learning offers tailored programs for three age groups: (1) preschool; (2) elementary school; and (3) middle school. For each age group, extensive curricular materials are available, including materials for teachers, family letters and take home activities, a toolkit for principals, and streaming media content. With respect to the preschool program, lessons are brief, taking approximately 5–7 minutes, and cover 5 key areas over the course of 28 weeks: skills for learning; empathy; emotion management; friendship skills and problem solving; and transitioning to Kindergarten. There is an additional child protection unit that also can be implemented, which includes 6 lessons focused on staying safe and safe/unsafe touches. Given the focus of this book is on peer victimization, we do not provide extensive details about this supplemental unit.

The newly designed elementary school program couples a social-emotional learning program with focused units on bullying prevention and child protection. In the social-emotional learning domain, students in Kindergarten to 5th grade have tailored sets of units (3–4 main units, depending on grade) that include from 22–25 lessons (also depending on grade). In Kindergarten to 3rd grade, units are focused on: skills for learning; empathy, emotional management; and problem solving. For students in grades 4–5, the 3 units are: empathy and skills learning; emotion management; and problem solving. The core programs are supplemented with 1 unit on bullying prevention that covers 4 key lessons. All students receive content on recognizing, reporting, and refusing bullying, and bystander power. For students in grades 4–5, they also review content on bystander responsibility, and cyber bullying and bystanders. Similar to the early childhood program, there is also a child protection unit, which is developmentally tailored to an elementary age population.

The middle school program is designed for pre-adolescents and adolescents, and materials associated with each 25-minute lesson are presented to students using a web-based portal. For 6th–8th graders, each of the 4 units have the same overarching themes: mindsets and goals; values and friendships; thoughts, emotions, and decisions; and serious peer conflicts. Across these units there are a total of 26 lessons, with optional review and assessment at the end of each of the units. There is some variability in lessons based on grade; for instance, students cover gender harassment in 7th grade, and discuss sexual harassment in 8th grade. A unique component of the middle school program is the availability of 200 advisory activities, given that middle schools are often structured in such a way that all students have advisory once or more per week. Three primary types of activities are provided: class challenges, class meetings (guided discussions), and service learning projects.

With respect to overall program effectiveness, Second Step was one of the programs featured in the National Registry of Evidence-Based Programs and Practices, which summarized that positive findings have been found for the program with respect to student climate; student social competency; bullying behaviors; bullying-related problems; and bystander behavior. A recent systematic review synthesized findings from across 24 studies evaluating Second Step (Moy & Hazen, 2018); studies included youth from Kindergarten through 8th grade. Researchers considered outcomes separately by research design, with analyses for randomized controlled trials, quasi-experimental designs, and single group repeated measures designs. In each case, there were three general outcome domains assessed: prosocial behaviors, antisocial behaviors, and knowledge. Broadly, results indicated that program participation was associated with increases in knowledge and prosocial behaviors, but was not related to antisocial indicators. Another recent meta-analysis, with a slightly larger sample of included studies ($n = 27$) also evaluated program effects for prosocial behaviors, antisocial behaviors, and knowledge, with attention to moderating effects (Moy et al., 2018). Researchers were particularly interested in evaluating whether program effects were similar across metro area and geographical contexts. Results were consistent with the prior meta-analysis, with strongest program effects for knowledge, small but significant effect on prosocial behaviors, and no statistically effects on antisocial behaviors. Importantly, program effects were similar regardless of metro area (e.g., rural vs. urban), and across countries.

These programs have been associated with increases in knowledge and prosocial behaviors

Some individual studies have evaluated specific programs within the broader suite of programs. The most limited information exists on the early learning program, given it was developed most recently. Emerging evidence suggests, however, that students who participate in the program demonstrate improvements in executive functioning, and marginally stronger social-emotional skills (Upshur et al., 2017). In terms of social-emotional skills, younger children demonstrated greater gains than older children. Authors speculated that one potential explanation for the minimal program effects on social-emotional skills was that given the developmental stage of children, control classrooms were also addressing social emotional skills, as is typical in preschool settings.

The elementary curriculum has been evaluated based on multiple editions of the program. Based on the 2012 program version, results from a randomized control trial indicated that there were few overall program effects for K–2 grade students who participated in the program across a 1-year period (Low et al., 2015). However, more nuanced analyses indicated that there were significant effects in multiple domains for students who at baseline had deficits in social-emotional functioning relative to their peers. For these youth, there were treatment effects for outcomes including prosocial behaviors, conduct problems, and emotion management. Note that in this evaluation the Second Step program was combined with a brief proactive classroom management training as well. Results from an early randomized control trial also suggested that 3rd–6th grade students in the intervention group demonstrated positive changes in beliefs about bystander responsibilities (Frey et al., 2005).

With respect to the middle school curriculum, a randomized control trial was conducted across a 2-year period in 36 schools from Illinois and Kansas. Findings following the first year of program implementation among 6th grade students indicated that there were significant reductions in physical aggression for youth in intervention schools compared to control schools (Espelage et al., 2013). Specifically, students in schools that had implemented Second Step were 42% less likely to endorse using physical aggression than their peers at control schools. However, intervention effects were not found for bullying involvement (victimization or perpetration), homophobic teasing, or sexual violence. Results published after the second year of program implementation indicated that for students in Illinois schools only, those in the intervention schools reported being targeted less frequently by homophobic name calling, and less sexual harassment perpetration, relative to their peers at control schools (Espelage et al., 2015). However, there were no differences between intervention and control school outcomes on bullying victimization, bullying perpetration, or physical aggression.

Given the salience of implementation factors, researchers have evaluated which factors were most predictive of strong program implementation (defined as adherence and engagement), and the association between implementation and outcomes, for an earlier version of Second Step (Low et al., 2013). Key findings from this study indicated that a number of factors were significantly associated with program engagement, but not adherence. Specifically, school climate and rates of students eligible for free and reduced price lunch were significantly associated with student engagement, with engagement lower at schools in which more students were eligible for free and reduced price lunch. Further, student engagement was associated with program outcomes including bullying victimization.

4.4.4 Key Elements Across Effective Programs

A number of key elements across effective programs can be gleaned from what is known to date. Drawing from reviews and meta-analyses on bullying prevention programs, as well as other theoretical and empirical publications in this area, yields valuable information on the approaches and components that tend to be associated with more effective programs. For instance, there is strong support for a social-ecological approach. This means that multiple environments need to be considered – from various school contexts (e.g., the school as a whole; the classroom), to the community to home (Hong & Espelage, 2012). It may be that additional adjunctive programming efforts are needed that extend outside the school context, for example that provide parents training or increasing awareness about bullying and best practices in responding among community members (Bradshaw, 2015; Holt et al., 2013). Optimal interventions take a whole school approach, are longer in duration, and cover a greater scope (Rigby, 2008; Ttofi & Farrington, 2011; Vreeman & Carroll, 2007). From a similar contextual framework, Leff (2007) has recommended the use of participatory action research for assurance that prevention implementation is both evidence-based and meets the specific needs of the local community. In sum, as advocated by the National Academies of Sciences, Engineering and Medicine's Committee on the Biological and Psychosocial Effects of Peer Victimization, the most effective prevention efforts are school-wide and include multiple components, and such efforts should continue to be subjected to rigorous evaluations to determine their effects in large student samples (Flannery et al., 2016).

Key aspects for success: a social-ecological and whole-school approach, with systematic monitoring of implementation and greater fidelity

Aspects without any effect, or negative effects, on bullying include: peer mediation, zero tolerance policies, and assemblies

With respect to specific program features, several components of school-wide programs are associated with greater effectiveness, including parent meetings, firm disciplinary methods, better playground supervision, classroom management, teacher training, cooperative learning, and schools' readiness to implement school-wide programs (Ttofi & Farrington, 2011). In contrast, Evans and colleagues (2014) highlighted that programs using innovative and creative approaches (e.g., using an interactive video game) seemed to be more likely to result in changes in bullying behaviors. For particular subgroups of students – such as victimized youth – additional research needs to be conducted to determine which program components and practices are particularly helpful to them (Juvonen et al., 2016). Importantly, elements have also been identified that appear to have negative effects on bullying in school, including peer mediation, zero tolerance policies, and assemblies (Flannery et al., 2016; Ttofi & Farrington, 2011).

Finally, authors of reviews and meta-analyses have pointed to core implementation features across programs associated with greater efficacy, including systematic monitoring of program implementation (Smith et al., 2004) and fidelity (Farrington & Ttofi, 2009). The necessity of high quality implementation is echoed across school safety research more broadly (Astor et al., 2010). Two particularly salient implementation aspects are duration and intensity; research indicates both are associated with decreasing bullying perpetration and victimization (Farrington & Ttofi, 2009; Ttofi & Farrington, 2011).

4.5   Problems in Carrying Out the Treatments

As described above, implementation plays a central role in the effectiveness of bullying prevention programs, and without high-quality implementation schools will likely not observe desired program effects (American Educational Research Association, 2013). At times, given school charactenistics and dynamics, it can be challenging to implement a program with complete fidelity. Similarly, it is necessary for there to be buy in from administrators to teachers, or it is likely the program will not be rolled out with sufficient fidelity. Further, bullying prevention programs can be costly, rendering them out of reach for some schools. For instance, Second Step offers a K–5 bundle that includes the social emotional learning program and bullying prevention unit for $3,419. A schoolwide license for the middle school program costs $2,749 for one year. Program developers note that Second Step meets requirements for federal and state grant funding that schools might choose to pursue (https://www.secondstep.org/funding-grants).

4.6 Summary

Research suggests that bullying prevention programs collectively have demonstrated only modest effects. Further, research has highlighted the importance of taking into account developmental stage when selecting programs, as elements that are effective vary between children and adolescents. Across all programs, implementation fidelity is a critical component. Finally, with respect to specific programs, three of the most widely implemented and evaluated are the Olweus Bullying Prevention Program, KiVa, and Second Step Social-Emotional Learning. Materials are available online for each of these programs that schools can review to determine the degree to which they fit with schools' needs.

5

Case Vignette

Let's return to the case of Maria mentioned in the introduction. She is the 7th-grade girl who first experienced cyberbullying by her peers and then in-person peer victimization when her peers gossiped about her and posted a sign calling her a "slut." June, a school psychologist, has been tasked with handling the situation. At first, June feels overwhelmed at the thought as her only knowledge of the incident comes third hand. Patel, a 7th-grade science teacher had told June that he overheard two students whispering about a sign on Maria's locker. When June enters the 7th-grade hallway, she finds students mulling around and giggling. On the floor, she finds a crumpled-up sign that says, "Maria is a slut" in red ink. June assumes that the sign refers to Maria, the new 7th grader, and sets out to find her. June finally finds Maria sitting outside the girls' bathroom with her sweatshirt over her head. June reintroduces herself as she only met Maria briefly at the start of the year. Maria does not respond. June sits down next to Maria and tries to build some rapport before asking Maria about the sign, which June has tucked in her pocket. June tells Maria that she can see that she is upset and she would like to help her. Noting that it is lunch time, June invites Maria to join her in her office for lunch. Maria reluctantly agrees.

In an effort to increase Maria's comfort, June inquiries about mundane topics, such as Maria's favorite lunch as they walk to June's office. Once Maria has eaten her lunch and is comfortably sitting in June's office, June begins to ask Maria some questions about the incident. Although June, an experienced psychologist, has suspicions about what occurred earlier in the day, she refrains from sharing these assumptions. Instead, she says, "Maria, I could see that you were really upset earlier and my job as the school's psychologist is to look after everyone's well-being. I would like to hear what happened and see if there are any ways that I can help you feel better or resolve the issue." Maria nods and says, "Okay, but will you promise not to tell anyone? My parents would be so angry if they found out about what happened." Maria's request, a common one among adolescents, gives June some pause. On the one hand, June needs to find out what happened today; on the other hand, she cannot promise that she will not tell anyone. June validates Maria's fear about her parents and notes that she cannot make that promise because her job requires her to look out for the well-being and safety of students, but she can promise that she will keep Maria informed about what steps June needs to take.

Comforted by June's honesty, Maria begins recounting the events of earlier in the day. She explains how Jessica and her friends had tricked Maria into thinking she was communicating with a boy in their grade, but actually it was Jessica, Sarah, and Jasmine using a fake Instagram account. Maria is unwilling to share what specifically she communicated over Instagram, but she does recount how she was repeatedly asked to disclose personal details, which Jessica later shared multiple times with other students. Maria states that she overheard students whispering about her and then found the sign on her locker and only later was able to piece everything together when she heard other girls talking about it in the bathroom. June listens intently and starts to identify the repeated pattern of victimization that Jessica and the other girls carried out against Maria over Instagram. June has dealt with bullying cases before and is aware that her school, like schools in most states, has a specific bullying policy and procedure. When Maria finishes explaining the situation, June validates how upsetting the situation is, reminds Maria that regardless of what she shared online, she did not deserve to have her private conversations repeated, and thanks her for disclosing what happened, acknowledging how important and brave it was for Maria to talk with a trusted adult. She tells Maria that she wants to spend some time figuring out the best way to move forward with the situation and explains that she will need to discuss the situation with a few other staff members. After checking that Jessica and the other girls are not in Maria's next two classes, June asks Maria if she is comfortable returning to class or if she would like to spend the afternoon in the guidance counselor's waiting room. Maria decides that she would like to attend her remaining two classes as she has art, which is her favorite class, and then a study hall. June reminds Maria that she can come back at any time and encourages her to stay away from Jessica and the other girls for the time being. She also explains the importance of Maria not trying to hurt or seek retaliate toward the girls.

June reviews her school's bullying procedure, which states that school staff need to talk to multiple people about the incident and both the families of the target and aggressor need to be notified of the incident. Recognizing that she will need to speak to the accused aggressors and a few other students, June enlists the help of the vice principal and head of the English Department, who co-wrote the school's bullying plan and procedure as mandated by the state. As June walks to the main office, she is stopped by another teacher who updates her on what the teacher overheard in the cafeteria. The teacher describes a similar story to the one that Maria offered. June thanks the teacher for relaying the information and assures her that the situation is being handled. June also asks the teacher to reassure any students that ask about the incident that the school staff know about it and are responding to it. After updating the vice principal and head of the English Department on the bullying incident, they create a plan to separately meet with the alleged aggressors as this has been documented to be a best practice. Careful to not cause further harm to Maria, none of them mention her as the reporter of the incident. They refer to Maria's account as well as the information provided from the two teachers anonymously when meeting with the aggressors.

When questioning Sarah, who was involved in creating the fake account and circulating the contents of the conversation between Maria and the fake account, June does not immediately provide details of the incident that she has previously learned. Instead, she invites Sarah to share what happened earlier in the day. Through tears, Sarah explains what happened and admits to helping create the fake account, but denies creating or posting the sign on Maria's locker. June thanks Sarah for her honesty and at the same acknowledges how harmful her behavior was. June notes the school's student conduct policy and lets Sarah know she will face consequences for her actions. June goes on to explain that she will call Sarah's parents to inform them of the incident and asks Sarah whether she would like to be part of the phone call or if she would like June to call them alone. Sarah states that she would like June to call her parents alone. June explains that the consequences for Sarah's actions will be determined by school administrators by the end of the day and June will tell Sarah about them. June provides Sarah with a pass to return to class and instructs her to stay away from Maria, as well as the other girls involved in the incident. She also asks Sarah to delete all the messages she circulated and highlighted that she should not continue to send out information like that.

After meeting with Sarah, June finds the vice principal and head of the English Department to discuss their meetings with the other aggressors. Jasmine, like Sarah, openly discussed her role in the situation. Both girls had indicated that Jessica had thought of the idea and carried out most of the conversations with Maria through the fake account. Jessica denied being the one who thought of the idea, but by now several students and teachers had provided support for Sarah, Jasmine, and Maria's accounts of the incident. The vice principal, who had interviewed Jessica, noted that Jessica stated she was only involved because she wanted to have friends and she thought this would be a good way to make more. Reviewing the school's bullying policy together, the staff determined that the incident did in fact meet the criteria for bullying. In an effort to create consequences that help teach a lesson rather than simply punishing the aggressors with a suspension, which is not effective, the staff thought of projects that each aggressor could complete to better understand the impact of bullying and cyberbullying. Sarah will research and create posters that define cyberbullying and provide steps on how to prevent it. Jasmine will research how to identify bullying and how to help friends and peers who are being bullied. She will then create posters or a presentation on the information she learned. Jessica will read a book about bullying and write a summary of the book. In the summary, Jessica will identify what she learned in the book and what she can do differently next time. All girls will be required to meet with a school counselor for four sessions and after those sessions a reassessment will occur to understand whether they would benefit from additional counseling. During the individual sessions, the aggressors will work with the school counselor on how to apologize and make amends with Maria. This will be a collaborative approach, and none of the aggressors will be forced to apologize immediately as this is rarely effective.

After outlining the consequences, each staff member finds the aggressor they interviewed and explains the consequences. While meeting with Sarah, June emphasizes that the consequences are intended to help Sarah understand the impact of her actions and help foster a supportive school community. June explains that she will call Sarah's parents to explain the situation and associated consequences. At the end of the meeting, June reminds Sarah that this action does not define her and she has an opportunity to improve her relationships and contribute to a stronger school community. June calls Sarah's parents and explains the situation. June provides Sarah's parents with the facts, again being careful to not mention Maria as one of the sources. June also refers Sarah's parents to the school's student conduct handbook and reminds them to not reach out to any students or parents about this incident. June outlines the consequences for Sarah and explains the rationale behind the consequences and leaves time for Sarah's parents to ask questions. June ends the call similar to her meeting with Sarah by emphasizing that Sarah is a valuable member of the school community and the school hopes that Sarah will learn and grow from this incident.

Before the day ends, June finds Maria to check-in. When meeting privately in June's office, Maria reports that she has not received any more messages from the girls. June informs Maria that all of the aggressors have been spoken to and have received consequences to help them improve their behavior. June again thanked Maria for sharing what happened and encouraged Maria to continue speaking up. June also explained that given Maria was the recipient of such harmful behavior, she will be encouraged to continue checking-in with June. Lastly, June asked Maria whether she wanted to stay in June's office while she called Maria's parents or if she wanted June to call them alone. Maria requested to stay in the office and June invited her to explain the situation to her parents with June offering support and clarification when needed. June again emphasized Maria's braveness in coming forward and how the school was handling the situation with the intent of creating a safer school environment. As with Sarah's parents, June referred Maria's parents to the school's student conduct handbook and emphasized that they should refrain from reaching out to any students or parents of students involved in the incident.

In June's future individual meetings with the girls, she would ask them questions beyond the scope of this one incident to better understand any potential social skills or problem-solving deficits that could be improved through the teaching and practice of skills. Examples of interview questions she may ask are included in Appendix 3.

6

Further Reading

Espelage, D. L., & Swearer, S. M. (Eds.) (2011). *Bullying in North American schools* (2nd ed.). Routledge.
Includes information on understanding and responding to bullying using a social-ecological perspective. Reviews relevant literature on bullying and offers suggestions and recommendations for educators on how to select and implement a bullying prevention program that responds to individual schools' unique ecology.

Kowalski, R. M., Limber, S. P., Agatston, P. W. (2012). *Cyberbullying: Bullying in the digital age* (2nd ed.). Wiley.
Reviews cyberbullying research and laws and policies related to cyberbullying. Includes a chapter outlining what educators can do in response to cyberbullying, as well as a chapter on what parents can do in response to cyberbullying.

Goldblum, P., Espelage, D. L., Chu, J., & Bongar, B. (2014). *Youth suicide and bullying: Challenges and strategies for prevention and intervention.* Oxford University Press. https://doi.org/10.1093/med:psych/9780199950706.001.0001
Examines the theories relating to bullying and suicide. Provides recommendations for educators and parents on how to respond to these educational and public health concerns. Delves into the research examining differences in the prevalence and relationship between bullying and suicide among ethnic, sexual, and gender minority youth.

PREVNet Book Series: https://www.prevnet.ca/node/1079
Four volumes about bullying prevention curated by leading bullying researchers in Canada. The first volume includes information on bullying prevention in both Canada and internationally. The second volume focuses on bullying prevention programs in schools and understanding the contexts which shape students' behaviors and responses. The third volume spotlights bullying across the lifespan and lays out how all individuals can play a role in responding to and preventing bullying. The fourth volume expands beyond bullying to include information on how to best support the development of healthy relationships, with a specific focus on Aboriginal youth and socially just approaches.

7

References

Aboujaoude, E., Savage, M., Starcevic, V., & Salame, W. (2015). Cyberbullying: Review of an old problem gone viral. *Journal of Adolescent Health, 57*(1), 10–18. https://doi.org/10.1016/j.jadohealth.2015.04.011

Achenbach, T. M., & Rescorla, L. A. (2001). *Manual for the ASEBA School-Age Forms & Profiles*. University of Vermont.

American Educational Research Association. (2013). *Prevention of bullying in schools, colleges, and universities: Research report and recommendations.* https://www.aera.net/Portals/38/docs/News%20Release/Prevention%20of%20Bullying%20in%20Schools,%20Colleges%20and%20Universities.pdf

American Psychiatric Association. (2013). *Diagnostic and statistical manual of mental disorders: DSM-5*. https://doi.org/10.1176/appi.books.9780890425596

Astor, R. A., Guerra, N., & Van Acker, R. (2010). How can we improve school safety research? *Educational Researcher, 39,* 69–78. https://doi.org/10.3102/0013189X09357619

Austin, S. & Joseph, S. (1996). Assessment of bully/victim problems in 8 to 11 year-olds. *British Journal of Educational Psychology, 66,* 447–456. https://doi.org/10.1111/j.2044-8279.1996.tb01211.x

Bacchini, D., Esposito, G., & Affuso, G. (2009). Social experience and school bullying. *Journal of Community & Applied Social Psychology, 19*(1), 17–32. https://doi.org/10.1002/casp.975

Bandura, A. (1986). *Social foundations of thought and action: A social cognitive theory.* Prentice-Hall.

Barlett, C. (2017). From theory to practice: Cyberbullying theory and its application to intervention. *Computers in Human Behavior, 72,* 269–275. https://doi.org/10.1016/j.chb.2017.02.060

Barlett, C., Gentile, D., & Chew, C. (2016). Predicting cyberbullying from anonymity. *Psychology of Popular Media Culture, 5*(2), 171–180. https://doi.org/10.1037/ppm0000055

Beckman, L., & Svensson, M. (2015). The cost-effectiveness of the Olweus Bullying Prevention Program: Results from a modeling study. *Journal of Adolescence, 45,* 127–137. https://doi.org/10.1016/j.adolescence.2015.07.020

Bellmore, A., Huang, H. C., Bowman, C., White, G., & Cornell, D. (2017). The trouble with bullying in high school: Issues and considerations in its conceptualization. *Adolescent Research Review, 2*(1), 11–22. https://doi.org/10.1007/s40894-016-0039-7

Benbenishty, R., & Astor, R. (2005). *School violence in context culture, neighborhood, family, school, and gender.* Oxford University Press.

Berger, C., & Rodkin, P. (2012). Group influences on individual aggression and prosociality: Early adolescents who change peer affiliations. *Social Development, 21*(2), 396–413. https://doi.org/10.1111/j.1467-9507.2011.00628.x

Bernstein, J. Y., & Watson, M. W. (1997). Children who are targets of bullying: A victim pattern. *Journal of Interpersonal Violence, 12,* 483–498. https://doi.org/10.1177/088626097012004001

Bond, L., Wolfe, S., Tollit, M., Butler, H., & Patton, G. (2007). A comparison of the Gatehouse Bullying Scale and the Peer Relations Questionnaire for Students in Secondary School. *Journal of School Health, 77*(2), 75–79. https://doi.org/10.1111/j.1746-1561.2007.00170.x

Bontempo, D. E., & D'Augelli, A. R. (2002). Effects of at-school victimization and sexual orientation on lesbian, gay, or bisexual youths' health risk behavior. *Journal of Adolescent Health, 30*(5), 364–374. https://doi.org/10.1016/S1054-139X(01)00415-3

Bowes, L., Arseneault, L., Maughan, B., Taylor, A., Caspi, A., & Moffitt, T. (2009). School, neighborhood, and family factors are associated with children's bullying involvement: A nationally representative longitudinal study. *Journal of the American Academy of Child & Adolescent Psychiatry, 48*(5), 545–553. https://doi.org/10.1097/CHI.0b013e31819cb017

Bowlby, J. (1973). *Attachment and loss. Vol. 2 Separation anxiety and anger.* Basic Books.

Bradshaw, C. (2015). Translating research to practice in bullying prevention. *American Psychologist, 70*, 322–332. https://doi.org/10.1037/a0039114

Bronfenbrenner, U. (1977). Toward an experimental ecology of human development. *American Psychologist, 32*(7), 513–531. https://doi.org/10.1037/0003-066X.32.7.513

Bussey, K., & Bandura, A. (1999). Social cognitive theory of gender development and differentiation. *Psychological Review, 106*(4), 676–713. https://doi.org/10.1037/0033-295X.106.4.676

Calvert, S., Appelbaum, M., Dodge, K., Graham, S., Hall, G., Hamby, S., Fasig-Caldwell, L. G., Citkowicz, M., Galloway, D. P., & Hedges, L. (2017). The American Psychological Association Task Force assessment of violent video games: Science in the service of public interest. *American Psychologist, 72*(2), 126–143. https://doi.org/10.1037/a0040413

Casey-Cannon, S., Hayward, C., & Gowen, K. (2001). Middle-school girls' reports of peer victimization: Concerns, consequences, and implications. *Professional School Counseling, 5*(2), 138-147.

Cassidy, J., Kirsh, S., Scolton, K., & Parke, R. (1996). Attachment and representations of peer relationships. *Developmental Psychology, 32*(5), 892–904. https://doi.org/10.1037/0012-1649.32.5.892

Cassidy, J., & Shaver, P. R. (2016). *Handbook of attachment: Theory, research, and clinical applications* (3rd ed.). The Guilford Press.

Centers for Disease Control and Prevention. (2019). *Youth Risk Behavior Surveillance System – YRBSS data.* https://www.cdc.gov/healthyyouth/data/yrbs/index.htm

Chan, J. H. F., Myron, R. R., & Crawshaw, C. M. (2005). The efficacy of non-anonymous measures of bullying. *School Psychology International, 26*(4), 443–458. https://doi.org/10.1177/0143034305059020

Chen, L., Ho, S., & Lwin, M. (2017). A meta-analysis of factors predicting cyberbullying perpetration and victimization: From the social cognitive and media effects approach. *New Media & Society, 19*(8), 1194–1213. https://doi.org/10.1177/1461444816634037

Chester, K. L., Spencer, N. H., Whiting, L., & Brooks, F. M. (2017). Association between experiencing relational bullying and adolescent health-related quality of life. *Journal of School Health, 87*(11), 865–872. https://doi.org/10.1111/josh.12558

Connolly, I., & O'Moore, M. (2003). Personality and family relations of children who bully. *Personality and Individual Differences, 35*(3), 559–567. https://doi.org/10.1016/S0191-8869(02)00218-0

Cook, C. R., Williams, K. R., Guerra, N. G., Kim, T. E., & Sadek, S. (2010). Predictors of bullying and victimization in childhood and adolescence: A meta-analytic investigation. *School Psychology Quarterly, 25*(2), 65–83. https://doi.org/10.1037/a0020149

Copeland, W. E., Wolke, D., Angold, A., & Costello, E. J. (2013). Adult psychiatric outcomes of bullying and being bullied by peers in childhood and adolescence. *JAMA Psychiatry, 70*(4), 419–426. https://doi.org/10.1001/jamapsychiatry.2013.504

Craig, W. M., Pepler, D., & Atlas, R. (2000). Observations of bullying in the playground and in the classroom. *School Psychology International, 21*, 22–36. https://doi.org/10.1177/0143034300211002

Crawford, A., & Manassis, K. (2011). Anxiety, social skills, friendship quality, and peer victimization: An integrated model. *Journal of Anxiety Disorders, 25*(7), 924–931. https://doi.org/10.1016/j.janxdis.2011.05.005

Crick, N. R., & Grotpeter, J. K. (1995). Relational aggression, gender, and social-psychological adjustment. *Child Development, 66*, 710–722. https://doi.org/10.2307/1131945

Eisenberg, M. E., Neumark-Sztainer, D., & Story, M. (2003). Associations of weight-based teasing and emotional well-being among adolescents. *Archives of Pediatric and Adolescent Medicine, 157*(8), 733–738. https://doi.org/10.1001/archpedi.157.8.733

Espelage, D. L., Basile, K. C., De La Rue, L., & Hamburger, M. E. (2015). Longitudinal associations among bullying, homophobic teasing, and sexual violence perpetration among middle school students. *Journal of Interpersonal Violence, 30*(14), 2541–2561. https://doi.org/10.1177/0886260514553113

Espelage, D., Bosworth, K., & Simon, T. (2000). Examining the social context of bullying behaviors in early adolescence. *Journal of Counseling & Development, 78*(3), 326–333. https://doi.org/10.1002/j.1556-6676.2000.tb01914.x

Espelage, D., & Holt M. (2001). Bullying and victimization during early adolescence: Peer influences and psychosocial correlates. *Journal of Emotional Abuse, 2,* 123–42. https://doi.org/10.1300/J135v02n02_08

Espelage, D. L., Low, S., Polanin, J. R., & Brown, E. C. (2013). The impact of a middle school program to reduce aggression, victimization, and sexual violence. *Journal of Adolescent Health, 53*(2), 180–186. https://doi.org/10.1016/j.jadohealth.2013.02.021

Espelage, D. L., Low, S., Polanin, J., & Brown, E. (2015). Clinical trial of Second Step middle-school program: Impact on aggression & victimization. *Journal of Applied Developmental Psychology, 37,* 52–63. https://doi.org/10.1016/j.appdev.2014.11.007

Espelage, D. L., Low, S., Van Ryzin, M. J., & Polanin, J. R. (2015). Clinical trial of Second Step Middle School Program: Impact on bullying, cyberbullying, homophobic teasing, and sexual harassment perpetration. *School Psychology Review, 44,* 464–479. https://doi.org/10.17105/spr-15-0052.1

Evans, S., Davies, C., & DiLillo, D. (2008). Exposure to domestic violence: A meta-analysis of child and adolescent outcomes. *Aggression and Violent Behavior, 13*(2), 131–140. https://doi.org/10.1016/j.avb.2008.02.005

Evans, C. B. R., Fraser, M. W., & Cotter, K. L. (2014). The effectiveness of school-based bullying prevention programs: A systematic review. *Aggression and Violent Behavior, 19,* 532–544. https://doi.org/10.1016/j.avb.2014.07.004

Farrell, A., Henry, D. B., & Bettencourt, A. (2013). Methodological challenges examining subgroup differences: Examples from universal school-based youth violence prevention trials. *Prevention Science, 14*(2), 121–133. https://doi.org/10.1007/s11121-011-0200-2

Farrell, A. K., Simpson, J. A., & Rothman, A. J. (2015). The relationship power inventory: Development and validation. *Personal Relationships, 22*(3), 384–413. https://doi.org/10.1111/pere.12072

Farrington, D. P., Gaffney, H. Lasel, F., & Ttofi, M. M. (2017). Systematic reviews of the effectiveness of developmental prevention programs in reducing delinquency, aggression, and bullying. *Aggression and Violent Behavior, 33,* 91–106. https://doi.org/10.1016/j.avb.2016.11.003

Ferguson, C. J., San Miguel, C., Kilburn, J. C., & Sanchez, P. (2007). The effectiveness of school-based anti-bullying programs: A meta-analytic review. *Criminal Justice Review, 32*(4), 401–414. https://doi.org/10.1177/0734016807311712

Farrington, D. P., & Ttofi, M. M. (2009). Reducing school bullying: Evidence based implications for policy. *Crime and Justice, 38*(1), 281–345. https://doi.org/10.1086/599198

Festinger, L. (1957). *A theory of cognitive dissonance.* Stanford University Press. https://doi.org/10.1515/9781503620766

Fitzpatrick, K. M., Dulin, A. J., & Piko, B. F. (2007). Not just pushing and shoving: School bullying among African American adolescents. *Journal of School Health, 77*(1), 16–22. https://doi.org/10.1111/j.1746-1561.2007.00157.x

Flannery, D. J., Todres, J., Bradshaw, C. P., Amar, A. F., Graham, S., Hatzenbuehler, M., Masiello, M., Moreno, M., Sullivan, R., Vaillancourt, T., Le Menestrel, S. M., & Rivara, F. (2016). Bullying prevention: A summary of the Report of the National Academies of Sciences, Engineering, and Medicine. *Prevention Science, 17*(8), 1044–1053.

Forsberg, C., Wood, L., Smith, J., Varjas, K., Meyers, J., Jungert, T., & Thornberg, R. (2018). Students' views of factors affecting their bystander behaviors in response to school bullying: A cross-collaborative conceptual qualitative analysis. *Research Papers in Education, 33*(1), 127–142.

Franco, K., Rothman, E. F., & Temple, J. R. (in press). *Dating violence.* Hogrefe Publishing.

Frey, K. S., Nolen, S. B., Edstrom, L. V. S., & Hirschstein, M. K. (2005). Effects of a school-based social-emotional competence program: Linking children's goals, attributions, and behavior. *Journal of Applied Developmental Psychology, 26*(2), 171–200. https://doi.org/10.1016/j.appdev.2004.12.002

Friedman, M. S., Marshal, M. P., Guadamuz, T. E., Wei, C., Wong, C. F., Saewyc, E. M., & Stall, R. (2011). A meta-analysis of disparities in childhood sexual abuse, parental physical abuse, and peer victimization among sexual minority and sexual nonminority individuals. *American Journal of Public Health, 101*(8), 1481–1494. https://doi.org/10.2105/AJPH.2009.190009

Furlong, M. J., Sharkey, J. D., Felix, E. D., Tanigawa, D., & Green, J. G. (2010). Bullying assessment: A call for increased precision of self-reporting procedures. In S. R. Jimerson, S. M. Swearer, & D. L. Espelage (Eds.), *Handbook of bullying in schools: An international perspective* (pp. 329–345). Routledge.

Gini, G. (2006). Social cognition and moral cognition in bullying: What's wrong? *Aggressive Behavior, 32*(6), 528–539. https://doi.org/10.1002/ab.20153

Gini, G. & Pozzoli, T. (2013). Bullied children and psychosomatic problems: A meta-analysis. *Pediatrics, 132*(4), 720–729. https://doi.org/10.1542/peds.2013-0614

Gini, G., Pozzoli, T., & Hymel, S. (2014). Moral disengagement among children and youth: A meta-analytic review of links to aggressive behavior. *Aggressive Behavior, 40*(1), 56–68. https://doi.org/10.1002/ab.21502

Gladden, M. R., Vivolo-Kantor, A. M., Hamburger, M. E., & Lumpkin, C. D. (2014). *Bullying surveillance among youth: Uniform definitions for public health and recommended data elements, Version 1.0.* https://www.cdc.gov/violenceprevention/pdf/bullying-definitions-final-a.pdf

Goncy, E. A., Sutherland, K. S., Farrell, A. D., Sullivan, T. N., & Doyle, S. T. (2015). Measuring teacher implementation in delivery. *Prevention Science, 16*(3), 440–450. https://doi.org/10.1007/s11121-014-0508-9

Gotthiel, N. F., & Dubow, E. F. (2001). The interrelationships of behavioral indices of bully and victim behavior. *Journal of Emotional Abuse, 2*, 75–93. https://doi.org/10.1300/J135v02n02_06

Green-Hennessey, S. (2018). Suspension of the National Registry of Evidence-Based Programs and Practices: The importance of adhering to the evidence. *Substance Abuse Treatment, Prevention, and Policy, 13*, Article 26. https://doi.org/10.1186/s13011-018-0162-5

Grills, A., & Holt, M. (2017). Child and adolescent disorders. In S. G. Hofmann (Ed.), *Clinical psychology: A global perspective* (pp. 135–152). Wiley.

Grills, A. E., & Ollendick, T. H. (2000). *Peer victimization and internalizing symptoms in children* [Unpublished master's thesis]. Virginia Tech.

Guo, S. (2016). A meta-analysis of the predictors of cyberbullying perpetration and victimization. *Psychology in the Schools, 53*(4), 432–453. https://doi.org/10.1002/pits.21914

Haataja, A., Voeten, M., Boulton, A. J., Ahtola, A., Poskiparta, E., & Salmivalli, C. (2014). The KiVa antibullying curriculum and outcome: Does fidelity matter? *Journal of School Psychology, 52*, 479–493. https://doi.org/10.1016/j.jsp.2014.07.001

Hamburger, M. E., Basile, K. C., & Vivolo, A. M. (2011). *Measuring bullying victimization, perpetration, and bystander experiences: A compendium of assessment tools.* Centers for Disease Control and Prevention, National Center for Injury Prevention and Control. https://www.cdc.gov/violenceprevention/pdf/bullycompendium-a.pdf https://doi.org/10.1037/e580662011-001

Harris, J. (2009). *The nurture assumption: Why children turn out the way they do* (revised & updated edition). Free Press.

Hatzenbuehler, M. L., Duncan, D., & Johnson, R. (2015). Neighborhood-level LGBT hate crimes and bullying among sexual minority youths: A geospatial analysis. *Violence and Victims, 30*(4), 663–675. https://doi.org/10.1891/0886-6708.VV-D-13-00166

Hawker, D. S. J., & Boulton, M. J. (2000). Twenty years' research on peer victimization and psychosocial maladjustment: A meta-analytic review of cross-sectional studies. *Journal of Child Psychology and Psychiatry and Allied Disciplines, 41*(4), 441–455. https://doi.org/10.1111/1469-7610.00629

Hill, C., & Holly, K. (2011). *Crossing the line: Sexual harassment at school*. AAUW. https://www.aauw.org/app/uploads/2020/03/Crossing-the-Line-Sexual-Harassment-at-School.pdf

Hirsh, J., Galinsky, A., & Zhong, C. (2011). Drunk, powerful, and in the dark: How general processes of disinhibition produce both prosocial and antisocial behavior. *Perspectives on Psychological Science, 6*(5), 415–427. https://doi.org/10.1177/1745691611416992

Holcomb, W. R. (2010). *Sexual violence*. Hogrefe Publishing.

Holt, M. K., Green, J. G., Reid, G., DiMeo, A., Espelage, D., Felix, E. D., Furlong, M. J., Paul Poteat, V., & Sharkey, J. D. (2014). Associations between past bullying experiences and psychosocial and academic functioning among college students. *Journal of American College Health, 62*(8), 552-560. https://doi.org/10.1080/07448481.2014.947990

Holt, M. K., Kaufman Kantor, K., & Finkelhor, D. (2009). Parent/child concordance about bullying involvement and family characteristics related to bullying and peer victimization. *Journal of School Violence, 8*, 42–63. https://doi.org/10.1080/15388220802067813

Holt, M., Matjasko, J., Espelage, D., Reid, G., & Koenig, B. (2013). Sexual risk taking and bullying among adolescents. *Pediatrics, 132*(6), E1481–1487. https://doi.org/10.1542/peds.2013-0401

Holt, M., Raczynski, K., Frey, K., Hymel, S., & Limber, S. (2013). School and community-based approaches for preventing bullying. *Journal of School Violence, 12*, 238–252. https://doi.org/10.1080/15388220.2013.792271

Holt, M. K., Vivolo-Kantor, A. M., Polanin, J. R., Holland, K. M., Degue, S., Matjasko, J. L., Wolfe, M., & Reid, G. (2015). Bullying and suicidal ideation and behaviors: meta-analysis. *Pediatrics, 135*(2), e496–509. https://doi.org/10.1542/peds.2014-1864

Hong, J. S., & Espelage, D. L. (2012). A review of research on bullying and peer victimization in school: An ecological system analysis. *Aggression and Violent Behavior, 17*(4), 311–322. https://doi.org/10.1016/j.avb.2012.03.003

Hutchings, J., & Clarkson, S. (2015). Introducing and piloting the KiVa bullying prevention programme in the UK. *Educational and Child Psychology, 32*, 49–61.

Jaffe, P. G., Wolfe, D. A., & Campbell, M. (2012). *Growing up with domestic violence*. Hogrefe Publishing.

Jiménez-Barbero, J., Ruiz-Hernandez, Llor-Zaragoza, Parez-Garcia, & Llor-Esteban. (2016). Effectiveness of anti-bullying school programs: A meta-analysis. *Children and Youth Services Review, 61*, 165–175. https://doi.org/10.1016/j.childyouth.2015.12.015

Jolliffe, D., & Farrington, D. (2011). Is low empathy related to bullying after controlling for individual and social background variables? *Journal of Adolescence, 34*(1), 59–71. https://doi.org/10.1016/j.adolescence.2010.02.001

Johns, M. M., Lowry, R., Andrzejewski, J., Barrios, L. C., Demissie, Z., McManus, T., Rasberry, C. N., Robin, L., & Underwood, J. M. (2019). Transgender identity and experiences of violence victimization, substance use, suicide risk, suicide behaviors, and sexual risk behaviors among high school students – 19 states and large urban school districts, 2017. *Morbidity and Mortality Weekly Report, 68*(3), 67–71.

Juvonen, J., Nishina, A., & Graham, S. (2000). Peer harassment, psychological adjustment, and school functioning in early adolescence. *Journal of Educational Psychology, 92*(2), 349–359. https://doi.org/10.1037/0022-0663.92.2.349

Juvonen, J., Schacter, H. L., Sainio, M., & Salmivalli, C. (2016). Can a school-wide bullying prevention program improve the plight of victims? Evidence for risk intervention effects. *Journal of Consulting and Clinical Psychology, 84*(4), 334–344. https://doi.org/10.1037/ccp0000078

Kaltiala-Heino, R., Rimpela, M., Marttunen, M., Rimpela, A., & Rantanen, P. (1999). Bullying, depression, and suicidal ideation in Finnish adolescents: School survey. *British Medical Journal, 319*, 348–351. https://doi.org/10.1136/bmj.319.7206.348

Kann, L., McManus, T., Harris, W. A., Shanklin, S. L., Flint, K. H., Hawkins, J., Queen, B., Lowry, R., O'Malley Olsen, E., Chyen, D., Whittle, L., Thornton, J., Lim, C., Yamakawa, Y., Brener, N., & Zaza, S. (2016). Youth risk behavior surveillance – United States, 2015. *Morbidity and Mortality Weekly Report: Surveillance Summaries, 65*(6), 1–174.

Kärnä, A., Voeten, M., Little, T., Alanen, E., Poskiparta, E., & Salmivalli, C. (2013). Effectiveness of the KiVa antibullying program: Grades 1–3 and 7–9. *Journal of Educational Psychology, 105*, 535–551. https://doi.org/10.1037/a0030417

Kärnä, A., Voeten, M., Little, T. D., Poskiparta, E., Kaljonen, A., & Salmivalli, C. (2011). A large scale evaluation of the KiVa antibullying program: Grades 4–6. *Child Development, 82*(1), 311–330. https://doi.org/10.1111/j.1467-8624.2010.01557.x

Kaufman, J., Birmaher, B., Axelson, D., Pereplitchikova, F., Brent, D., & Ryan, N. (2016). *K-SADS-PL DSM-5*. Kennedy Krieger Institute. https://www.kennedykrieger.org/sites/default/files/library/documents/faculty/ksads-dsm-5-screener.pdf

Kaukiainen, A., Salmivalli, C., Lagerspetz, K., Tamminen, M., Vauras, M., Mäki, H., & Poskiparta, E. (2002). Learning difficulties, social intelligence, and self-concept: Connections to bully–victim problems. *Scandinavian Journal of Psychology, 43*(3), 269–278. https://doi.org/10.1111/1467-9450.00295

Kelly, E. V., Newton, N. C., Stapinski, L. A., Slade, T., Barrett, E. L., Conrod, P. J., & Teesson, M. (2015). Suicidality, internalizing problems and externalizing problems among adolescent bullies, victims and bully-victims. *Preventive Medicine, 73*, 100–105. https://doi.org/10.1016/j.ypmed.2015.01.020

Kert, A. S., Codding, R. S., Tryon, G. S., & Shiyko, M. (2010). Impact of the word "bully" on the reported rate of bullying behavior. *Psychology in the Schools, 47*(2), 193–204. https://doi.org/10.1002/pits.20464

Kljakovic, M., & Hunt, C. (2016). A meta-analysis of predictors of bullying and victimisation in adolescence. *Journal of Adolescence, 49*, 134–145. https://doi.org/10.1016/j.adolescence.2016.03.002

Klomek, A. B., Marrocco, F., Kleinman, M., Schonfeld, I. S., & Gould, M. S. (2007). Bullying, depression, and suicidality in adolescents. *Journal of the American Academy of Child & Adolescent Psychiatry, 46*(1), 40-49. https://doi.org/10.1097/01.chi.0000242237.84925.18

Klomek, A. B., Sourander, A., Kumpulainen, K., Piha, J., Tamminen, T., Moilanen, I., Almqvist, F., & Gould, M. S. (2008). Childhood bullying as a risk for later depression and suicidal ideation among Finnish males. *Journal of Affective Disorders, 109*(1–2), 47–55. https://doi.org/10.1016/j.jad.2007.12.226

Kosciw, J. G., Greytak, E. A., & Diaz, E. M. (2009). Who, what, where, when, and why: Demographic and ecological factors contributing to hostile school climate for lesbian, gay, bisexual, and transgender youth. *Journal of Youth and Adolescence, 38*(7), 976–988. https://doi.org/10.1007/s10964-009-9412-1

Kowalski, R. M., Limber, S. P., & Agatston, P. W. (2012). *Cyberbullying: Bullying in the digital age* (2nd ed.). Wiley-Blackwell.

Lai, T., & Kao, G. (2018). Hit, robbed, and put down (but not bullied): Underreporting of bullying by minority and male students. *Journal of Youth and Adolescence, 47*, 619–635. https://doi.org/10.1007/s10964-017-0748-7

Lapidot-Lefler, N., & Barak, A. (2012). Effects of anonymity, invisibility, and lack of eye-contact on toxic online disinhibition. *Computers in Human Behavior, 28*(2), 434–443. https://doi.org/10.1016/j.chb.2011.10.014

Leff, S. S. (2007). Bullying and peer victimization at school: Considerations and future directions. *School Psychology Review, 36*(3), 406–412. https://doi.org/10.1080/02796015.2007.12087931

Lereya, S. T., Samara, M., & Wolke, D. (2013). Parenting behavior and the risk of becoming a victim and a bully/victim: A meta-analysis study. *Child Abuse & Neglect, 37*, 1091–1108. https://doi.org/10.1016/j.chiabu.2013.03.001

Limber, S. P. (2006). The Olweus Bullying Prevention Program: An overview of its implementation and research basis. In S. R. Jimerson & M. Furlong (Eds.), *Handbook of school violence and school safety: From research to practice*. (pp. 293–307). Lawrence Erlbaum Associates Publishers.

Limber, S. P., Olweus, D., Wang, W., Masiello, M., & Breivik, K. (2018). Evaluation of the Olweus Bullying Prevention Program: A large scale study of U.S. students in grades 3–11. *Journal of School Psychology, 69*, 56–72. https://doi.org/10.1016/j.jsp.2018.04.004

Lovegrove, P. J., Henry, K. L., & Slater, M. D. (2012). Examination of the predictors of latent class typologies of bullying involvement among middle school students. *Journal of School Violence, 11*(1), 75–93. https://doi.org/10.1080/15388220.2011.631447

Low, S., Cook, C., Smolkowski, K., & Buntain-Ricklefs, J. (2015). Promoting social-emotional competence: Evaluation of the elementary version of Second Step. *Journal of School Psychology, 53,* 463–477. https://doi.org/10.1016/j.jsp.2015.09.002

Low, S., Van Ryzin, M. J., Brown, E. C., Smith, B. H., & Haggerty, K. P. (2013). Engagement matters: Lessons from assessing classroom implementation of steps to respect: A bullying prevention program over a one-year period. *Prevention Science, 15*(2), 165–176. https://doi.org/10.1007/s11121-012-0359-1

Lund, E. M., & Ross, S. W. (2017). Bullying perpetration, victimization, and demographic differences in college students: A review of the literature. *Trauma, Violence, & Abuse, 18,* 348–360. https://doi.org/10.1177/1524838015620818

Ma, L., Phelps, E., Lerner, J. V., & Lerner, R. M. (2009). The development of academic competence among adolescents who bully and who are bullied. *Journal of Applied Developmental Psychology, 30*(5), 628–644. https://doi.org/10.1016/j.appdev.2009.07.006

Merrell, K. W., Gueldner, B. A., Ross, S. W., & Isaac, D. M. (2008). How effective are school bullying intervention programs? A meta-analysis of intervention research. *School Psychology Quarterly, 23*(1), 26–42. https://doi.org/10.1037/1045-3830.23.1.26

Mitsopoulou, E., & Giovazolias, T. (2015). Personality traits, empathy and bullying behavior: A meta-analytic approach. *Aggression and Violent Behavior, 21,* 61–72. https://doi.org/10.1016/j.avb.2015.01.007

Modecki, K. L., Minchin, J., Harbaugh, A. G., Guerra, N., & Runions, K. (2014). Bullying prevalence across contexts: A meta-analysis measuring cyber and traditional bullying. *Journal of Adolescent Health, 55*(6), 602–611. https://doi.org/10.1016/j.jadohealth.2014.06.007

Moon, B., & Alarid, L. (2015). School bullying, low self-control, and opportunity. *Journal of Interpersonal Violence, 30*(5), 839–856. https://doi.org/10.1177/0886260514536281

Morris, E. B., Zhang, B., & Bondy, S. J. (2006). Bullying and smoking: examining the relationships in Ontario adolescents. *Journal of School Health, 76*(9), 465–470. https://doi.org/10.1111/j.1746-1561.2006.00143.x

Mouttapa, M., Valente, T., Gallaher, P., Rohrbach, L., & Unger, J. (2004). Social network predictors of bullying and victimization. *Adolescence, 39,* 315–335.

Moy, G., & Hazen, A. (2018). A systematic review of the Second Step program. *Journal of School Psychology, 71,* 18–41. https://doi.org/10.1016/j.jsp.2018.10.006

Moy, G., Polanin, J. R., McPherson, C., & Phan, T.V. (2018). International adoption of the Second Step program: Moderating variables in treatment effects. *School Psychology International, 39,* 333–359. https://doi.org/10.1177/0143034318783339

Mynard, H., & Joseph, S. (2000). Development of the multidimensional peer-victimization scale. *Aggressive Behavior, 26,* 169–178. https://doi.org/10.1002/(SICI)1098-2337(2000)26:2<169::AID-AB3>3.0.CO;2-A

Nakamoto, J., & Schwartz, D. (2009). Is peer victimization associated with academic achievement? A meta-analytic review. *Social Development, 19*(2), 221–242. https://doi.org/10.1111/j.1467-9507.2009.00539.x

Nansel, T. R., Overpeck, M., Pilla, R. S., Ruan, W. J., Simons-Morton, B., & Scheidt, P. (2001). Bullying behaviors among US Youth: Prevalence and association with psychosocial adjustment. *JAMA, 285*(16), 2094–2100. https://doi.org/10.1001/jama.285.16.2094

Niemelä, S., Brunstein-Klomek, A., Sillanmäki, L., Helenius, H., Piha, J., Kumpulainen, K., Moilanen, I., Tamminen, T., Almqvist, F., & Sourander, A. (2011). Childhood bullying behaviors at age eight and substance use at age 18 among males. A nationwide prospective study. *Addictive Behaviors, 36*(3), 256-260. https://doi.org/10.1016/j.addbeh.2010.10.012

Nocentini, A., Fiorentini, G., Di Paola, L., & Menesini, E. (2019). Parents, family characteristics and bullying behavior: A systematic review. *Aggression and Violent Behavior, 45,* 41–50. https://doi.org/10.1016/j.avb.2018.07.010

Nocentini, A., & Menesini, E. (2016). KiVa anti-bullying program in Italy: Evidence of effectiveness in a randomized control trial. *Prevention Science, 17*, 1012–1023. https://doi.org/10.1007/s11121-016-0690-z

Olweus, D. (1993). Victimization by peers: Antecedents and long-term consequences. In K. H. Rubin & J. B. Asendorpf (Eds.), *Social withdrawal, inhibition, and shyness in childhood* (pp. 315–341). Lawrence Erlbaum.

Olweus, D. (1996). *Revised Olweus Bully/Victim Questionnaire*. Research Center for Health Promotion, University of Bergen, Norway.

Olweus, D. (2005). A useful evaluation design, and effects of the Olweus Bullying Prevention Program. *Psychology, Crime & Law, 11*(4), 389–402. https://doi.org/10.1080/10683160500255471

Olweus, D. (2011). Bullying at school and later criminality: Findings from three Swedishcommunity samples of males. *Criminal Behavior and Mental Health, 21*(2), 151–156. https://doi.org/10.1002/cbm.806

Orpinas, P. (1993). *Skills training and social influences for violence prevention in middle schools: A curriculum evaluation* [Doctoral dissertation, University of Texas-Houston, School of Public Health]. Dissertation Abstracts International, 94-01778.

Orpinas, P., & Horne, A. M. (2006). *Bullying prevention: Creating a positive school climate and developing social competence*. American Psychological Association.

Pabian, S., & Vandebosch, H. (2016). An investigation of short-term longitudinal associations between social anxiety and victimization and perpetration of traditional bullying and cyberbullying. *Journal of Youth and Adolescence, 45*(2), 328–339. https://doi.org/10.1007/s10964-015-0259-3

Parada, R. H. (2000). *Adolescent Peer Relations Instrument: A theoretical and empirical basis for the measurement of participant roles in bullying and victimization of adolescence: An interim test manual and a research monograph: A test manual*. Publication Unit, Self-concept Enhancement and Learning Facilitation (SELF) Research Centre, University of Western Sydney.

Patchin, J. W. & Hinduja, S. (2015). Defining cyberbullying: Implications for research. *Aggression and Violent Behavior, 23*, 69–74. https://doi.org/10.1016/j.avb.2015.05.013

Pellegrini, A. (2008). The roles of aggressive and affiliative behaviors in resource control: A behavioral ecological perspective. *Developmental Review, 28*(4), 461–487. https://doi.org/10.1016/j.dr.2008.03.001

Perry, D. G., Kusel, S. J., & Perry, L. C. (1988). Victims of peer aggression. *Developmental Psychology, 24*, 807–814. https://doi.org/10.1037/0012-1649.24.6.807

Phillips, V. I., & Cornell, D. G. (2012). Identifying victims of bullying: Use of counselor interviews to confirm peer nominations. *Professional School Counseling, 15*(3), 123–131. https://doi.org/10.1177/2156759X1201500304

Pinquart, M. (2017). Associations of parenting dimensions and styles with externalizing problems of children and adolescents: An updated meta-analysis. *Developmental Psychology, 53*(5), 873–932. https://doi.org/10.1037/dev0000295

Polanin, J. R., Espelage, D. L., & Pigott, T. D. (2012). A meta-analysis of school-based bullying prevention programs' effects on bystander intervention behavior. *School Psychology Review, 41*(1), 47–65. https://doi.org/10.1080/02796015.2012.12087375

Pouwels, J., Salmivalli, C., Saarento, S., Berg, Y., Lansu, T., & Cillessen, A. (2018). Predicting adolescents bullying participation from developmental trajectories of social status and behavior. *Child Development, 89*(4), 1157–1176. https://doi.org/10.1111/cdev.12794

Pouwels, J., Souren, P., Lansu, T., & Cillessen, A. (2016). Stability of peer victimization: A meta-analysis of longitudinal research. *Developmental Review, 40*(C), 1–24. https://doi.org/10.1016/j.dr.2016.01.001

Pozzoli, T., Gini, G., & Vieno, A. (2012). Individual and class moral disengagement in bullying among elementary school children. *Aggressive Behavior, 38*(5), 378–388. https://doi.org/10.1002/ab.21442

Prinstein, M. J., Boergers, J., & Vernberg, E. M. (2001). Overt and relational aggression in adolescents: Social-psychological adjustment of aggressors and victims. *Journal of Clinical Child Psychology, 30*(4), 479–491. https://doi.org/10.1207/S15374424JCCP3004_05

Radliff, K. M., Wheaton, J. E., Robinson, K., & Morris, J. (2012). Illuminating the relationship between bullying and substance use among middle and high school youth. *Addictive Behaviors, 37*(4), 569–572. https://doi.org/10.1016/j.addbeh.2012.01.001

Raikes, H., & Thompson, R. (2008). Attachment security and parenting quality predict children's problem-solving, attributions, and loneliness with peers. *Attachment & Human Development, 10*(3), 319–344. https://doi.org/10.1080/14616730802113620

Reijntjes, A., Kamphuis, J. H., Prinzie, P., & Telch, M. J. (2010). Peer victimization and internalizing problems in children: A meta-analysis of longitudinal studies. *Child Abuse & Neglect: The International Journal, 34*(4), 244–252. https://doi.org/10.1016/j.chiabu.2009.07.009

Reynolds, C. R., & Kamphaus, R. W. (2015). *Behavior Assessment for Children – third edition (BASC-3)*. Pearson.

Reynolds, W. M. (2003). *Reynolds Bully Victimization Scales for Schools manual*. The Psychological Corporation.

Rigby, K. (2008). *Children and bullying: How parents and educators can reduce bullying at school*. Blackwell Publishing.

Robers, S., Zhang, A., Morgan, R. E., & Musu-Gillette, L. (2015). *Indicators of school crime and safety: 2014* (NCES 2015-072/NCJ 248036). National Center for Education Statistics, US Department of Education, and Bureau of Justice Statistics, Office of Justice Programs, US Department of Justice. Washington, DC. https://nces.ed.gov/pubs2015/2015072.pdf

Roberts, W. B., & Morotti, A. A. (2000). The bully as victim: Understanding bully behaviors to increase the effectiveness of interventions in the bully-victim dyad. *Professional School Counseling, 4*, 148–155.

Rose, C., & Gage, N. (2017). Exploring the involvement of bullying among students with disabilities over time. *Exceptional Children, 83*(3), 298–314. https://doi.org/10.1177/0014402916667587

Rothon, C., Head, J., Klineberg, E., & Stansfeld, S. (2011). Can social support protect bullied adolescents from adverse outcomes? A prospective study on the effects of bullying on the educational achievement and mental health of adolescents at secondary schools in East London. *Journal of Adolescence, 34*(3), 579–588. https://doi.org/10.1016/j.adolescence.2010.02.007

Sainio, M., Veenstra, R., Huitsing, G., & Salmivalli, C. (2011). Victims and their defenders: A dyadic approach. *International Journal of Behavioral Development, 35*(2), 144–151. https://doi.org/10.1177/0165025410378068

Salmivalli, C. (1999). Participant role approach to school bullying: Implications for interventions. *Journal of Adolescence, 22*(4), 453–459. https://doi.org/10.1006/jado.1999.0239

Salmivalli, C., Kärnä, A., & Poskiparta, E. (2011). Counteracting bullying in Finland: The KiVa program and its effects on different forms of being bullied. *International Journal of Behavioral Development, 35*(5), 405–411. https://doi.org/10.1177/0165025411407457

Salmivalli, C., & Voeten, M. (2004). Connections between attitudes, group norms, and behaviour in bullying situations. *International Journal of Behavioral Development, 28*, 246–258. https://doi.org/10.1080/01650250344000488

Salmon, G., James, A., Cassidy, E. L., & Javaloyes, M. A. (2000). Bullying a review: Presentations to an adolescent psychiatric service and within a school for emotionally and behaviourally disturbed children. *Clinical Child Psychology and Psychiatry, 5*, 563–579. https://doi.org/10.1177/1359104500005004010

Samnani, A.-K., & Singh, P. (2012). 20 years of workplace bullying research: A review of the antecedents and consequences of bullying in the workplace. *Aggression and Violent Behavior, 17*(6), 581–589. https://doi.org/10.1016/j.avb.2012.08.004

Schäfer, M., Korn, S., Smith, P. K., Hunter, S. C., Mora-Merchan, J., Singer, M. M., & Van der Meulen, K. (2004). Lonely in the crowd: Recollections of bullying. *British Journal of Developmental Psychology, 22*(3), 379–394. https://doi.org/10.1348/0261510041552756

Schneider, S., O'Donnell, L., Stueve, A., & Coulter, R. (2012). Cyberbullying, school bullying, and psychological distress: A regional census of high school students. *American Journal of Public Health, 102*(1), 171–177. https://doi.org/10.2105/AJPH.2011.300308

Scholte, R., Engels, R., Overbeek, G., de Kemp, R., & Haselager, G. (2007). Stability in bullying and victimization and its association with social adjustment in childhood and adolescence. *Journal of Abnormal Child Psychology, 35*(2), 217–228. https://doi.org/10.1007/s10802-006-9074-3

Schroeder, B. A., Messina, A., Schroeder, D., Good, K., Barto, S., Saylor, J., & Masiello, M. (2012). The implementation of a statewide bullying prevention program: Preliminary findings from the field and the importance of coalitions. *Health Promotion Practice, 13*(4), 489–495. https://doi.org/10.1177/1524839910386887

Schumann, L., & Craig, W., & Rosu, A. (2013). Minority in the majority: Community ethnicity as a context for racial bullying and victimization. *Journal of Community Psychology, 41*(8), 959–972. https://doi.org/10.1002/jcop.21585

Search Institute. (2016). *User guide for The Developmental Assets Profile.* https://www.search-institute.org/wp-content/uploads/2017/11/Fluid-DAP-User-Guide-1-2016.pdf

Sigurdson, J. F., Wallander, J., & Sund, A. M. (2014). Is involvement in school bullying associated with general health and psychosocial adjustment outcomes in adulthood? *Child Abuse & Neglect, 38*(10), 1607–1617. https://doi.org/10.1016/j.chiabu.2014.06.001

Slattery, L. (2019). *A functional approach to bullying prevention and reduction: The development and evaluation of the Functional Behavior Assessment for Bullying-Behavior in Schools (FABB-S).* ProQuest Dissertations Publishing.

Smith, J. D., Schneider, B. H., Smith, P. K., & Ananiadou, K. (2004). The effectiveness of whole-school antibullying programs: A synthesis of evaluation research. *School Psychology Review, 33*(4), 547–560. https://doi.org/10.1080/02796015.2004.12086267

Smokowski, P. R., & Kopasz, K.H. (2005). Bullying in school: An overview of types, effects, family characteristics, and intervention strategies. *Children & Schools, 27*(2), 101–110. https://doi.org/10.1093/cs/27.2.101

Solberg, M. E., & Olweus, D. (2003). Prevalence estimation of school bullying with the Olweus Bully/Victim Questionnaire. *Aggressive Behavior, 29*(3), 239–268. https://doi.org/10.1002/ab.10047

Sourander, A., Brunstein Klomek, A., Kumpulainen, K., Puustjarvi, A., Elonheimo, H., Ristkari, T., Tamminen, T., Moilanen, I., Piha, J., & Ronning, J. A. (2011). Bullying at age eight and criminality in adulthood: Findings from the Finnish Nationwide 1981 Birth Cohort Study. *Social Psychiatry and Psychiatric Epidemiology, 46*(12), 1211–1219. https://doi.org/10.1007/s00127-010-0292-1

Srabstein, J. C., Berkman, B. E., & Pyntikova, E. (2008). Antibullying legislation: A public health perspective. *Journal of Adolescent Health, 42*(1), 11–20. https://doi.org/10.1016/j.jadohealth.2007.10.007

Sullivan, T. N., Sutherland, K. S., Farrell, A. D., Taylor, K. A., & Doyle, S. T. (2017). Evaluation of violence prevention approaches among early adolescents: Moderating effects of disability status and gender. *Journal of Child and Family Studies, 26*(4), 1151–1163. https://doi.org/10.1007/s10826-016-0629-9

Swearer, S. M. (2001). *Bully Survey – youth version (BSY)* [Unpublished manuscript]. University of Nebraska – Lincoln.

Swearer, S. M., & Cary, P. T. (2003). Perceptions and attitudes toward bullying in middle school youth: A developmental examination across the bully/victim continuum. *Journal of Applied School Psychology, 19*, 63–79. https://doi.org/10.1300/J008v19n02_05

Swearer, S. M., Wang, C., Maag, J., Siebecker, A., & Frerichs, L. (2012). Understanding the bullying dynamic among students in special and general education. *Journal of School Psychology, 50*, 503–520. https://doi.org/10.1016/j.jsp.2012.04.001

Tarshis, T. P., & Huffman, L. C. (2007). Psychometric properties of the Peer Interactions in Primary School (PIPS) questionnaire. *Journal of Developmental and Behavioral Pediatrics, 28*(2), 125–132. https://doi.org/10.1097/01.DBP.0000267562.11329.8f

The Highmark Foundation. (2009). *Bullying prevention: A statewide collaborative that works.* https://www.chpdp.org/wp-content/uploads/2014/03/Bullying-Prevention-A-Statewide-Initiative-that-Works.pdf

The Highmark Foundation. (2012). *The cost benefit of bullying prevention: A first time analysis of savings.* https://www.chpdp.org/wp-content/uploads/2014/03/Cost-Benefit-Analysis.pdf

Thornberg, R., & Jungert, T. (2013). Bystander behavior in bullying situations: Basic moral sensitivity, moral disengagement and defender self-efficacy. *Journal of Adolescence, 36*(3), 475–483. https://doi.org/10.1016/j.adolescence.2013.02.003

Thornberg, R., Wänström, L., Hong, J., & Espelage, D. (2017). Classroom relationship qualities and social-cognitive correlates of defending and passive bystanding in school bullying in Sweden: A multilevel analysis. *Journal of School Psychology, 63*, 49–62. https://doi.org/10.1016/j.jsp.2017.03.002

Ttofi, M. M., & Farrington, D. P. (2011). Effectiveness of school-based programs to reduce bullying: A systematic and meta-analytic review. *Journal of Experimental Criminology, 7*(1), 27–56. https://doi.org/10.1007/s11292-010-9109-1

Unnever, J. & Cornell, D. (2003). Bullying, self-control, and ADHD. *Journal of Interpersonal Violence, 18,* 129–147. https://doi.org/10.1177/0886260502238731

Upshur, C. C., Heyman, M., & Wenz-Gross, M. (2017). Efficacy trial of Second Step Early Learning (SSEL) curriculum: Preliminary outcomes. *Journal of Applied Developmental Psychology, 50,* 15–25. https://doi.org/10.1016/j.appdev.2017.03.004

van Geel, M., Vedder, P., & Tanilon, J. (2014). Relationship between peer victimization, cyberbullying, and suicide in children and adolescents: A meta-analysis. *JAMA Pediatrics, 168*(5), 435–442. https://doi.org/10.1001/jamapediatrics.2013.4143

Veenstra, R., Lindenberg, S., Munniksma, A., & Dijkstra, J. K. (2010). The complex relation between bullying, victimization, acceptance, and rejection: Giving special attention to status, affection, and sex differences. *Child Development, 81*(2), 480–486. https://doi.org/10.1111/j.1467-8624.2009.01411.x

Veenstra, R., Lindenberg, S., Zijlstra, B. J. H., De Winter, A. F., Verhulst, F. C., & Ormel, J. (2007). The dyadic nature of bullying and victimization: Testing a dual-perspective theory. *Child Development, 78*(6), 1843–1854. https://doi.org/10.1111/j.1467-8624.2007.01102.x

Vernberg, E. M., Jacobs, A. K., & Hershberger, S. L. (1999). Peer victimization and attitudes about violence during early adolescence. *Journal of Clinical Child Psychology, 28*(3), 286–395.

Vreeman, R. C., & Carroll, A. E. (2007). A systematic review of school-based interventions to prevent bullying. *Archives of Pediatric and Adolescent Medicine, 161,* 78–88. https://doi.org/10.1001/archpedi.161.1.78

Walters, G., & Espelage, D. (2018). Hostility, anger, and dominance as mediators of the sibling aggression school fighting relationship: Mechanisms of violence generalization. *Psychology of Violence, 10*(1), 48–57. https://doi.org/10.1037/vio0000227

Wang, J., Iannotti, R. J., Luk, J. W., & Nansel, T. R. (2010). Co-occurrence of victimization from five subtypes of bullying: Physical, verbal, social exclusion, spreading rumors, and cyber. *Journal of Pediatric Psychology, 35*(10), 1103–1112. https://doi.org/10.1093/jpepsy/jsq048

Wang, J., Iannotti, R. J., & Nansel, T. R. (2009). School bullying among adolescents in the United States: Physical, verbal, relational, and cyber. *Journal of Adolescent Health 45*(4), 368–375. https://doi.org/10.1016/j.jadohealth.2009.03.021

Wang, J., Nansel, T. R., & Iannotti, R. J. (2011). Cyber and traditional bullying: Differential association with depression. *Journal of Adolescent Health, 48*(4), 415–417. https://doi.org/10.1016/j.jadohealth.2010.07.012

Warden, D., Cheyne, B., Christie, D., Fitzpatrick, H., & Reid, K. (2003) Assessing children's perceptions of prosocial and antisocial peer behaviour. *Educational Psychology, 23*, 547–567. https://doi.org/10.1080/0144341032000123796

Wekerle, C., Wolfe, D. A., Cohen, J. A., Bromberg, D. S., & Murray, L. (2019). *Childhood maltreatment* (2nd ed.). Hogrefe Publishing.

Wienke Totura, C., Mackinnon-Lewis, C., Gesten, E., Gadd, R., Divine, K., Dunham, S., & Kamboukos, D. (2009). Bullying and victimization among boys and girls in middle school: The influence of perceived family and school contexts. *The Journal of Early Adolescence, 29*(4), 571–609. https://doi.org/10.1177/0272431608324190

Williams, K. R., & Guerra, N.G. (2007). Prevalence and predictors of internet bullying. *Journal of Adolescent Health, 41*(6), S14–S21. https://doi.org/10.1016/j.jadohealth.2007.08.018

Williford, A., Boulton, A., Noland, B., Little, T. D., Kärnä, A., & Salmivalli, C. (2012). Effects of the KiVa anti-bullying program on adolescents' depression, anxiety, and perception of peers. *Journal of Abnormal Child Psychology, 40*(2), 289–300. https://doi.org/10.1007/s10802-011-9551-1

Williford, A. P., Carter, L. M., & Pianta, R. C. (2016). Attachment and school readiness. In J. Cassidy & P. Shaver (Eds.), *Handbook of attachment: Theory, research, and clinical applications* (3rd ed., pp. 966–982). The Guilford Press.

Wolke, D., Woods, S., Bloomfield, L., & Karstadt, L. (2000). The association between direct and relational bullying and behaviour problems among primary school children. *Journal of Child Psychology and Psychiatry, 41*(8), 989–1002.

Wright, M. F., & Li, Y. (2013). The association between cyber victimization and subsequent cyber aggression: The moderating effect of peer rejection. *Journal of Youth and Adolescence, 42*(5), 662–674. https://doi.org/10.1007/s10964-012-9903-3

Yeager, D. S., Fong, C. J., Lee, H. Y., & Espelage, D. L. (2015). Declines in efficacy of anti-bullying programs among older adolescents: Theory and a three-level meta-analysis. *Journal of Applied Developmental Psychology, 37*(1), 36–51. https://doi.org/10.1016/j.appdev.2014.11.005

Appendix: Tools and Resources

The materials on the following pages may be reproduced by the purchaser for personal/clinical use.
The printable, letter-sized PDFs can be downloaded free of charge from the Hogrefe website after registration.

Appendix 1: Websites, Apps, Events
Appendix 2: Assessment Measures for Bullying Perpetration and Victimization
Appendix 3: Interview Questions

How to proceed:

1. Create a user account (or, if you have already one, please log in)

For customers from the USA, Canada, and the rest of the world:
hgf.io/login-us

For European customers:
hgf.io/login-eu

2. Download your supplementary materials

Go to **My supplementary materials** in your account dashboard and enter the code below. You will automatically be redirected to the download area, where you can access and download the supplementary materials.

Code: B-ABD2QA

To make sure you have permanent direct access to all the materials, we recommend that you download them and save them on your computer.

Appendix 1: Websites, Apps, Events

Websites & Apps

Results First Clearinghouse Database

https://www.pewtrusts.org/en/research-and-analysis/data-visualizations/2015/results-first-clearinghouse-database
- Provides information on the effectiveness of social policy programs drawing from the collections of nine national clearinghouses

StopBullying.gov

https://www.stopbullying.gov/resources/get-help-now
- Website dedicated to stopping bullying that is supported by the United States federal government
- Has sections on facts about bullying, laws & policies, what you can do, what teens can do, as well as multiple video and social media resources

Promoting Relationships & Eliminating Violence Network (PREVNet)

https://www.prevnet.ca/bullying
- Canadian hub for information on bullying and prevention that includes sections for educators, parents, teens, and kids, as well as a facts and solutions section
- Also has an affiliated website dedicated to parenting in the digital age, which answers questions about cyberbullying and provides guidance on how to effectively monitor children's online activities (http://cyberbullying.primus.ca/)

PACER's National Bullying Prevention Center

https://www.pacer.org/bullying/
- Additional information about bullying—with a specific section on Bullying and Harassment of Students with Disabilities (https://www.pacer.org/bullying/resources/students-with-disabilities/)

The National Child Traumatic Stress Network

https://www.nctsn.org/what-is-child-trauma/trauma-types/bullying/nctsn-resources
- Has downloadable guides on bullying and cyberbullying, as well as a free webinar for school personnel on cyberbullying and trauma

KnowBullying Mobile App

Supported by the Substance Abuse and Mental Health Services Administration
https://store.samhsa.gov/product/knowbullying
- App for parents, caregivers, and educators that provides information on how to have effective conversations with children about bullying; allows the user to set reminders to talk with children about bullying; provides tips on how to recognize if your child or student is being bullied

Office of Juvenile Justice and Delinquency Prevention (OJJDP)

https://www.ojjdp.gov/mpg/Topic/Details/3
- Review of research on 10 antibullying prevention programs

Colorado Department of Education: Office of Learning Supports

https://www.cde.state.co.us/mtss/ebbullyingprograms
- Downloadable 2017 pdf reviewing evidence-based bullying prevention programs

Striving to Reduce Youth Violence Everywhere

Supported by the U.S. Centers for Disease Control and Prevention
https://vetoviolence.cdc.gov/apps/stryve/detail/selection
- Searchable guide for programs to prevent violence. Utilize the filter to search specifically for bullying programs
- Also created "A Comprehensive Technical Package for the Prevention of Youth Violence and Associated Risk Behaviors," which details strategies to prevent youth violence, including bullying https://www.cdc.gov/violenceprevention/pdf/yv-technicalpackage.pdf

Events

No Name Calling Week

Supported by Gay, Lesbian, Straight Education Network (GLSEN)
https://www.glsen.org/no-name-calling-week
- This is a week dedicated to ending name calling and bullying. Website provides suggestions on how to support and implement this week
- Also has a handout for school administrators on how to address bullying in schools https://www.glsen.org/sites/default/files/GLSEN-NNCW-School-Administrators-Steps-To-Address-Bullying.pdf

October is Bullying Prevention Month

https://www.stompoutbullying.org/campaigns/national-bullying-prevention-awareness-month
- Suggestions and activities in support of Bullying Prevention Month

DoSomething.org

https://www.dosomething.org/us/causes/bullying
- Non-profit dedicated to promoting young people committed to social change. Students can join ongoing causes started by other youth or create their own. Can search for bullying-related causes started by youth

See p. 63 for instructions on how to obtain the printable, letter-sized PDF.

Appendix 2: Assessment Measures for Bullying Perpetration and Victimization

As detailed in the book, it is important to assess for bullying perpetration and victimization at both the individual and school-level. For more information on why assessments are important and how to implement an assessment of bullying, visit https://www.stopbullying.gov/prevention/assess-bullying#Develop%20and%20Implement%20an%20Assessment

Below is a list of measures that assess bullying perpetration and victimization. When possible, a link to the measure is provided.

Many of the measures are copyrighted; however, you can review the majority of them for free in the CDC-supported *Measuring Bullying Victimization, Perpetration, and Bystander Experiences: A Compendium of Assessment Tools* by Hamburger et al., 2011, available at https://www.cdc.gov/violenceprevention/pdf/bullycompendium-a.pdf

Measure	Author(s)	Scale information	Age/grade range	Website
Adolescent Peer Relations Instrument	Parada, 2000	Bullying & Victimization (verbal, social, physical) 18 items each scale	Ages 12–17	Provided in the CDC compendium.
Gatehouse Bullying Scale	Bond et al., 2007	Victimization (overt and covert) 12 items	Ages 10–15	© 2007 Blackwell Publishing. Provided in the CDC compendium.
Multidimensional Peer Victimization Scale	Mynard & Joseph, 2000	Victimization (physical, verbal, social manipulation, property attacks) 16 items	Ages 11–16	Scale included in published article
Peer Experiences Questionnaire	Vernberg et al., 1999	Assesses victimization and attitudes concerning aggression/bullying 17 items	elementary–12th grade	http://users.sch.gr/euadamop/wordpress/wp-content/uploads/2016/04/PEQ-questionnaire.pdf
Peer Interactions in Primary School Questionnaire	Tarshis & Huffman, 2007	Bullying & Victimization 22 items	Ages 8–12	© 2007 Lippincott Williams & Wilkins (LWW). Provided in the CDC compendium.
Peer Victimization Scale	Austin & Joseph, 1996	Victimization 6 items	Ages 8–11	© 1996 The British Psychological Society. Provided in the CDC compendium.
Reduced Aggression/Victimization Scale	Orpinas & Horne, 2006	Bullying & Victimization (overt, relational) 12 items	Ages 8–12	Provided in the CDC compendium.
Revised Olweus Bully/Victim Questionnaire/Olweus Bullying Questionnaire	Olweus, 1996; Solberg & Olweus 2003	Assesses bullying, victimization, and related attitudes/areas 40 items	Grades 3–12	https://www.researchgate.net/publication/247979482_The_Olweus_BullyVictim_Questionnaire
Revised Peer Experiences Questionnaire	Prinstein et al., 2001	Assesses bullying, victimization, prosocial behaviors 9 items each scale	Grades 7–12	Scale included in published article
Reynolds Bullying/Victimization Scales for Schools	Reynolds, 2003	Assesses bullying of self and others, distress related to bullying, and anxiety about school violence 3 Scales: 46, 35, & 29 items	Grades 3–12	Not freely available. See https://www.pearsonassessments.com/store/usassessments/en/Store/Professional-Assessments/Behavior/Reynolds-Bullying-Victimization-Scales-For-Schools/p/100000032.html
School Life Survey	Chan et al., 2005	Bullying & Victimization (physical, verbal, relational) 24 items	Ages 8–12	© 2005 Sage Publications, Ltd. Provided in the CDC compendium.
School Relationships Questionnaire	Wolke et al., 2000	Bullying & Victimization (overt, verbal, relational) 20 items	Ages 6–9	Provided in the CDC compendium.
Setting the Record Straight	Gotthiel & Dubow, 2001	Bullying & Victimization 30 items	Ages 8–11	© 2001, The Haworth Press Inc. Provided in the CDC compendium.

8. Appendix: Tools and Resources

Measure	Author(s)	Scale information	Age/grade range	Website
The Bully Survey	Swearer, 2001	Bullying, Victimization, Bystander, & Attitudes varied items/rating formats	Ages 10–18	If you would like to use the English version of the Swearer Bully Surveys, please email sswearer@unl.edu.
University of Illinois Bully Scale	Espelage & Holt, 2001	Bullying & Victimization (bullying, physical fighting, victimization) 18 items	Ages 8–18	Available after login at https://app.secondstep.org/Portals/0/G3/BPU/Evaluation_Tools/IllinoisBullyScaleStudent.pdf
Victimization Scale	Orpinas, 1993	Victimization (overt) 10 items	Ages 10–15	Freely available at https://mmcp.health.maryland.gov/epsdt/healthykids/Documents/Victimization%20Scale_English_instructions.pdf

See p. 63 for instructions on how to obtain the printable, letter-sized PDF.

Appendix 3: Interview Questions

Name:	Date:	Notes
Social Support		
<ul><li>Some students feel like they have too many friends. Some students feel like they have too few friends. And some students feel like they have just the right number of friends. Which type of student are you? − And how many friends is that? − Are you friends mainly from school? Sports? Dance? Community organizations? Religious groups? Camp? − How often do you see your friends outside of school? Daily? Weekly? Monthly? − Do you feel like you can talk to your friends about anything that is happening in your life? For example, do you talk to your friends when you are upset? − How do you usually communicate with your friends? In-person? Via text, social media, phone calls?</li><li>Are there adults in your life that you trust (i.e., you feel like you could go to if you had a problem and they would help you)? − Can you tell me a little about these adults? Who are they? How do you know them? − Do you talk to these adults when you are upset?</li></ul>		
Social Issues		
<ul><li>How often do you have a problem, conflict, or disagreement with friends? Daily? Weekly? Monthly?</li><li>How often do you have a problem, conflict, or disagreement with someone you go to school with, but is not your friend? Daily? Weekly? Monthly?</li></ul>		
Interpersonal Effectiveness & Problem Solving Style		
<ul><li>If one of your friends made you mad or sad, would you tell them they hurt your feelings?</li><li>If another person at school who is not your friend made you mad or sad, would you tell them they hurt your feelings?</li><li>When you have a problem, conflict, or disagreement with a friend, how do you resolve it? − Do you hit, push, or punch your friend? − Do you tease your friend? − Do you post about the problem on social media? − Do you try to get other friends to take your side? − Do you apologize? − Do you ask an adult for help?</li></ul>		
Emotion Regulation Skills		
<ul><li>When you get really upset, how do you calm yourself down? − Tell other people that you are upset? − Wait to feel better? − Not talk to anyone?</li><li>When someone makes you mad or sad, do you say things that are mean or hurtful? − (If they say yes) Do you ever wish you had not said those things?</li><li>When someone makes you mad or sad, do you hit, punch, or push the other person?</li></ul>		
Attribution Style		
<ul><li>When something bad happens to you, who do you blame? Yourself? Others?</li><li>When you lose a game, do you think it is because you are not good enough? Or because the other team was better? Or the game is unfair?</li></ul>		

See p. 63 for instructions on how to obtain the printable, letter-sized PDF.

Empathy	
<ul><li>If you saw a friend crying, what would you do?<ul><li>– Ask them what is wrong?</li><li>– Ignore them?</li><li>– Wait for them to stop crying?</li></ul></li><li>If you saw a peer (not a friend) in school crying, what would you do?<ul><li>– Ask them what is wrong?</li><li>– Ignore them?</li><li>– Wait for them to stop crying?</li></ul></li><li>If you saw a friend being hit, pushed, or punched by another student, what would you do?<ul><li>– Push, hit, punch the other kid?</li><li>– Go tell a teacher?</li><li>– Ignore the situation?</li></ul></li><li>If you saw a peer (not a friend) in school being hit, pushed, or punched by another student, what would you do?<ul><li>– Push, hit, punch the other kid?</li><li>– Go tell a teacher?</li><li>– Ignore the situation?</li></ul></li><li>Do you think you have something in common with every one of your friends? With every student in your grade? With every student in your school?</li></ul>	
Family Conflict	
<ul><li>Who do you live with?</li><li>When someone is upset in your household, what do they do?<ul><li>– Do they ever hit, push, or punch anyone?<ul><li>• (If yes) How often does this happen? Daily? Weekly? Monthly?</li></ul></li><li>– Do they ever scream and yell?<ul><li>• (If yes) How often does this happen? Daily? Weekly? Monthly?</li></ul></li></ul></li><li>Do you worry about someone you live with hurting you?</li><li>How do you parents/guardians/caretakers respond if you get a low grade at school?</li><li>How do you parents/guardians/caretakers respond if you get in trouble at school?</li></ul>	

See p. 63 for instructions on how to obtain the printable, letter-sized PDF.